An Essay on

Secretary-General Nikai Toshihiro

A No.2 figure who surpasses No.1 figures /
A politician of peace, benevolence, and tolerance

Morita Minoru

R O N S O -

Preface

I think it is time to review the basic perspective of political analysis and research of political history.

When political researchers observe and analyze the movement of politics, most of them places No.1 politicians on the center; they have tried to see everything by making the movement of No.1 politicians their axis. However, it seems difficult to record true political movements by this "No.1" view of history.

History sometimes moves around No.2 figures, not No.1. A number of political reporters and researchers, though, ignore the presence of No.2 and try to explain political events through No.1 figures as the main axis. This is a crooked stereotype, and one has to amend such an attitude.

When observing, researching, and reporting, or when recording in a publication, one should overcome excessive obsession with the No.1 view of history.

A person who by profession reports the Japanese politics or bequeaths it as a record should be aware that the current Japanese politics, especially that of late Heisei era and early Reiwa era, have been moving around Nikai Toshihiro, Secretary-General of Liberal Democratic Party (LDP).

During major shifts in history, No.2 figures who have the power to move the history often appear.

Zhuge Liang Kongming of the "Three Kingdom" era of ancient China, Katsu Kaisyu of the end of Edo era and early days of Meiji era, Suzuki Kantaro of the end days of World War II, and Miki Bukichi, the main architect of the merger of the two conservative parties—all of them made bigger achievements than the No.1 figures and made the historical shift possible.

In the field of political history, there is a theory that "A powerful No.2 figure makes history", and I think it is true.

After World War II, Japan changed its political system and became a nation of parliamentary democracy. After that, some great No.2 figures appeared. As well as Miki Bukichi, such outstanding No.2 figures as Tanaka Kakuei, Ohira Masayoshi, Kanemaru Shin, and Nikai Toshihiro have flourished.

Among them, Tanaka and Ohira acted as No.2 just for a short period on their way to No.1. And though Kanemaru became a powerful No.2, he left almost nothing which can be called as a significant political achievement.

In the post-World War II period, only Miki and Nikai have been powerful politicians who persisted in the position of No.2 and made great political achievements.

From the end days of Showa era to Heisei and Reiwa era, Nikai Toshihiro, now Secretary-General of LDP, has been acting as a powerful No.2 figure. Though he occupies the position of No.2 in the current political arena of Japan, his ability is No.1.

When one looks through Nikai's political achievements, he will find they are remarkably big, such as constructing a tourism-and-culture-oriented country, establishing the Tsunami Disaster Prevention Basic Law, creating "World Tsunami Awareness Day" at United Nations, promoting a policy for disaster-prevention, disaster-reduction, and national resilience, and driving the peaceful, friendly diplomacy with such Asian countries as China, South Korea, and Vietnam, as well as Russia. There has never been a No.2 politician who has made such great achievements which go down in history. Thus, Nikai Toshihiro is one of the great No.2 politicians of modern Japan who are on par with Katsu Kaisyu, Suzuki Kanataro, and Miki Bukichi.

We have to review the politics of contemporary Japan, and I wrote this book thinking that one needs to describe Nikai, a powerful No.2 politician, exactly and based on the truth. This must be a responsibility of mine, who have engaged in the political analysis as a political commentator.

Here I ask you, the reader of this book, to discard a fixed notion and look at the truth about Nikai, an outstanding political leader whom we Japanese people can be proud of, without being hung up on the No.1 view of history.

This book contains testimonies of many persons. I not only interviewed with Japanese residents but went abroad several times and met with persons to obtain their testimonies.

I would like to thank them all for the interview.

I have heard all these precious testimonies directly, but I am responsible for the wording of them. Also, I (Morita Minoru) am responsible for everything in this book.

As this book is a record of the important facts about the political history of Japan, I omitted honorifics on the persons who appear in this book.

March 2020

At the library of my house
Morita Minoru

CONTENTS

Chapter 3 Nikai's political achievements which surpasses those of "No.1" figures

Introduction

Why I publish 'An Essay on Secretary-General Nikai Toshihiro' now

As of March 2020, Nikai Toshihiro, Secretary-General of Liberal Democratic Party (LDP), has held this position for a fourth consecutive term. During the 65 years since LDP was formed through the merger of the conservative parties in 1955, Nikai is the only Secretary-General who has held this position for a fourth consecutive term. Before Nikai, there have never been any Secretary-General who held the position for a fourth consecutive term, thus it is a new record. Therefore, it will not be exaggrating to say that Nikai is the best and brightest Secretary-General of LDP.

In the 65-years history of LDP, the one who held the position of General-Secretary for the longest period was Tanaka Kakuei. Tanaka, alternating with Fukuda Takeo, his political rival, acted as General-Secretary from 1960's to early 70's, and his tenure has been the longest until now. Though, in September 2020, Nikai broke this record.

In the past when Japan Socialist Party(JSP) was the biggest opposition party, the title of its No.2 (i.e. the Secretary-General of the party) was "書記長（Syoki-cho）", while that of LDP has been "幹事長（Kanji-cho）". But nowadays, all the parties in Japan use the title of "幹事長".

However, the Secretary-General of LDP and that of other parties varies greatly in their significance. The Secretary-General of LDP is practically the top executive who is totally responsible for managing Diet affairs, elections, and activities of the party in general. As the President of LDP focuses entirely on managing the government as the Prime Minister, the matters of the party are all entrusted on Secretary-General. The decision-maker of the activities of LDP is Secretary-General, so President, who is also Prime Minister, doesn't and cannot interfere with them. Meanwhile, in other parites, Secretary-Generals are just assistants of the head of the party.

It is supposed that Nikai's final goal as a politician has been becoming Secretary-General of LDP. It is widely agreed that Nikai aren't seeking any position above Secretary-General and has never done so. Therefore, in the elections of the President of LDP, power struggle for the position of Prime Minister will never occur with Nikai being its part. For President, if there is any possibility that "No.2", Secretary-General, would be his rival in the next election, neither his mind nor position as President and Prime Minister will not be stable.

Nikai, in exchange of stabilizing the position of Abe Shinzo, President of LDP and Prime Minister, has gotten freedom of action and the actual power as Secretary-General. Hayashi Motoo, Acting Secretary-General and best adviser to Nikai, said to me, "Since Mr. Nikai became Secretary-General, Prime Minister Abe has never interfered with him. Managing Diet issues, elections, and the operation of the Party - all of them has been entrusted to Secretary-General Nikai".

I think Hayashi's words are true, for he has been closest to Nikai and supported Nikai's activity. Nikai is the most powerful Secretary-General both in name and in reality.

I named this book "An Essay on Secretary-General Nikai Toshihiro" because I feel that Nikai has the nature of being not just Secretary-General of LDP, but of "the entire field of Japanese politics" and has built up achievements appropriate for it. Nikai is the best statesman whom one can call "Secretary-General of we Japanese people", and this title contains this subjective view of mine.

It is true that the tenure of Nikai as the Secretary-General lasts forever, and may come to end on September 2020 at the earliest. Despite it, the fourth consecutive term and the longest tenure as Secretary-General of LDP, achieved on September, is still a surprising record. He will be recorded and remembered as "the greatest Secretary-General in the history of Japanese politics".

Nikai became a member of the Diet in 1983 and has being winning the twelve consecutive elections. Even on the Lower House election 30th of August in 2009, when the Democratic Party of Japan took power, Nikai kept his seat in his own constituency. He is extremely good at election. He never lost his seat. When the general election in 2009, he faced ferocious attacks, but he was resilient. Since he has no weaknesses, even if he was under personal attacks, his position is utterly tenable.

As I will discuss this issue later in this book, Nikai is a remarkable politician in terms of ethics, intelligence, and the sense of unity with people.

Most politicians seek to be prime minister. But Nikai is not interested in it, has never been pursuing more than No.2 status, and has been trying to do his best to turn his creeds and ideals into reality.

I want many politicians to learn his way of life. One of my aims in this book is to teach young politicians that to pursue the top job is not the only purpose of politicians and that "Nikai's way of being No.2" is also worthwhile.

The subtitle of this book is "平和・博愛・忠恕の政治家（a politician of peace, benevolence, and tolerance）". In this, I would like to show that Nikai is a politician of total pacifism and benevolence, and who has limitless kindness and caring toward the entire nation and all humanity. And "忠恕（tolerance）" is a word found in 'Analects' and means limitless caring for citizens.

In modern times, some great "No.2" figures appeared at the arena of Japanese politics - Katsu Kaisyu of the end days of Edo era and the early days of Meiji era, Suzuki Kantaro of the end of the World War II, and Miki Bukichi of the period of merging the conservative parties. I will describe the concept of "No.2" in detail, and I think Nikai is not only on par with these historical "No.2" politicians but outstrip them.

I hope that many young politicians seek to become a "No.2 politician" like Katsu Kaisyu, Suzuki Kantaro, Miki Bukichi, and Nikai Toshihiro. Being "No.1" doesn't have to be their prime goal, as these

"No.2" politicians outstrip "No.1" figures in historical achievements. And this is proved by the history.

Young people who aspire to be a politician can learn a lot of from Nikai's political life. Furthermore, not only to politicians but also to many people who want to live for the world and people, his way of life can be a precious guiding principle for their lives.

His ethical and simple private life, strong love for his native land, complete awareness of peace, democratic sense of politics, strong egalitarianism which never conforms with unfair discrimination, sense of unity with ordinary citizens, way of life to spare no effort, and undauntable optimism—these are the things on which young politicians and those who are responsible for the next generation should base their direction of life, and I hope they see the way of Nikai as an ideal standard as a politician and a human.

From the political life of Nikai, one can learn that even if he never becomes a "No.1" as a politician, he can work sufficiently for people and humankind. In addition, I hope this book be used as a textbook by all those who are embarking on a political path for the happiness and prosperity of humankind.

Chapter 1

The real pictures of Nikai Toshihiro, who always acts up to the "with the people" attitude and "pacifism"

1. The energetic daily life of Nikai

On February 8th 2020, I accompanied Nikai Toshihiro, Secretary-General, and Hayashi Motoo, Acting Secretary-General, to cover their study tour and campaign stop directly. We departed Tokyo station at 10 a.m., and returned to Tokyo at 11 p.m. During this hard schedule, I kept looking at the true image of Nikai.

His activity in Choshi city (Chiba Prefecture) began with a lunch party held upon his arrival on 12:30. After the addresses by Hayashi and Koshikawa Shinichi, the mayor of the city, Nikai made a short speech and encouraged the people of Choshi, saying strongly "Without the advancement of Choshi city, there is no advancement of Chiba Prefecture, and without the advancement of Chiba Prefecture, there is no advancement of Japan. I am ready to support the advancement of Choshi city at full power". Strain and cheering followed it.

For Nikai, it was hard after this. While I, sitting next to Nikai, enjoyed fresh seafood of Choshi, he had no time to enjoy the seafood in front of him, as dozens of people came up to greet him, each holding his or her business card. Nikai shook hands with each of them, exchanged their business cards, and listened to them, all the while looking at their eyes. He kept treating each one of them politely, so he could not enjoy his food. When he finally extended his hand to the chopsticks, he was asked to be photographed with. Nikai accepted it with a smile. Everyone wanted to be photographed with Nikai, and Nikai accepted all of it. After finishing photographing, Nikai picked up his chopsticks again, but it was time to depart for the next destination. He could enjoy only half of his food.

We toured five places, and it was really hard; at every place, people was waiting to make a petition to Nikai. He listened to their petitions and appeals intently. Sometimes, he called his secretary to take a memo, and discussed with the accompanying officials of the central government. He was classifying things which could be handled soon and the ones which should be considered carefully, and making necessary instructions quickly. He got no rest; he didn't seem fatigue at all, though he is 80 years old now.

I was surprised that he sincerely faced every single person. He talked with them in the same level and treated them equally and wholeheartedly.

In a market, Nikai visited each shop and listened to the shop masters. He was checking the economic conditions of this city with his own eyes. And, though not so many, he purchased something with his own money. He never made light of anyone; his attitude toward the shopkeepers were full of kindness and caring.

In the evening, Nikai attended "A get-together with Hayashi Motoo, a member of the Lower House" and made a speech.

"Hayashi Motoo, Acting Secretary-General and my close ally, is working at the heart of the Japanese politics and will be an important person in the future. The next Lower House election will take place soon, but Hayashi will not be able to visit his own constituency because he directs the election as Acting Secretary-General. So I ask every one of you to support him".

This speech was mixed with humor and enthusiasm, and really great. It won the hearts and minds of the audience, and laughter arose among them often. From this speech, the citizens of Choshi learned how deep the relationship between Nikai and Hayashi is, and how strong their bond is.

According to the original schedule, we must have departed to Tokyo one hour earlier, but Nikai still had a big task as Secretary-General of LDP. It was an interview with dozens of reporters who cover Secretary-General exclusively. Nikai talked with them for about two hours; he takes care of these reporters, for he always acts up to the belief that everyone is the same as a human being.

In the car on the way home, there were only Nikai and me. Remembering Nikai's energetic activity, I said to him, "I recalled the energetic activity of Tanaka Kakuei back in the New Year reception of

1974 held in the Prime Minister's Office. Tanaka, then Prime Minister, shook hands, talked with, and greeted each one of more than 1,000 guests. Your energetic activities today reminded me of Prime Minister Tanaka".

On the way back to Tokyo, we stopped at service areas, and Nikai visited the shops each time. He talked with every single shopkeeper, asked about the condition of their business, and purchased something with his own money. He cheered up them, who were working until late at night. Nikai shows respect to everyone he meets, and encourages him. He never gets rest; he is really a man.

When we finally arrived in Tokyo, Nikai offered to send me back home first. I firmly declined it and parted with him at the public dormitory for Diet members in Akasaka, but his secretary sent me my home. It was past 11 p.m.

Through the trip to Choshi city, I saw Nikai's energetic activities in which he showed respect to everyone and treated them humbly, and I realized the extraordinariness of Nikai as a politician.

Nikai is always kind and gentle to everyone; he never speaks a word which would hurt somebody. Caring is in Nikai's words at all time.

A verse "Kind words bring life" in the Old Testament is a maxim which everyone should respect.

About 30 years ago, I visited various places in Wakayama Prefecture with Nikai. Back then, Nikai treated everyone kindly. Not only in Wakayama Constituency No.3, which has been his own constituency, but also in Constituency No.1 and No.2, his attitude of respecting people never changed.

30 years have passed since then, but Nikai Toshihiro, now Secretary-General of LDP, always treats everyone kindly and respects them. Nikai is always humble.

In fact, on the night before this trip to Choshi, Nikai accepted my proposal of reporting, and interviewed with me for about 3 hours. During this, he kept answering to my questions sincerely.

Before meeting with me, Nikai visited the Chinese Embassy with

Saito Tetsuo, the Secretary-General of Komeito, Hayashi Motoo, Acting Secretary-General of Liberal Democratic Party, and Koizumi Ryuji, the head of international division of LDP, to interview with Kong Xuanyou, Ambassador of China to Japan. There, Nikai made this speech.

"As for the situation of pneumonia infection by the outspread of Covid-19 virus, Japan takes it seriously, and I express my deepest sympathies over the Chinese people. Now, China is trying hard to prevent and control the outspread. As with the famous saying, "A friend in need is a friend indeed", Japan will call upon the power of all Japanese people, go all out to provide every support to China, and counter the outspread of infection with China. I assert that everything is possible if China and Japan cooperate closely. We can defeat the infection. We will deliver the 125,000 pieces of protective clothing which we have collected so far to Hubei, Zhejiang, and Guangdong province as soon as possible".

Nikai always works hard. Two days later, he flew to Kyusyu to talk with the representatives of agriculture-related organizations. Nikai never takes rest; he always walks with Japanese people, works for them, and kept working to protect the world peace.

2. Nikai Toshihiro, a statesman who have always acted up to pacifism and made great achievements

Nikai Toshihiro is a great pacifist and genuine democrat.

If asked what is the most important thing in this world, I would answer that it is peace.

During the 75 years since World War II ended, I have been believing that the most important thing in this world is peace, and assessed politicians based on their attitude toward the "peace".

In the field of politics, the most important thing is to defend peace. The true value of a politician is determined by whether he is making efforts for peace. When I evaluate a politician, I focus above all on whether he is a pacifist. And the reason I respect Nikai Toshihiro is that he is a genuine pacifist.

Among media personnel, it is widely believed that conservative politicians of Japan are not so enthusiastic about defending peace, and their ardor for peace is not so strong as that of opposition party politicians. It is, though, a prejudice and a wrong fixed notion. One should not forget that there are true pacifists even among conservative politicians, such as Nikai.

Tanaka Kakuei, Ohira Masayoshi, Gotoda Masaharu, and Kanemaru Shin were all pacifists. And so are all the politicians of Komeito. It is true that when Japan Socialist Party still existed, many of the opposition party politicians claimed to be a pacifist. However, since the name of JSP disappeared and a system of two conservative parties was established, the difference between LDP and opposition parties has almost disappeared, and one of its reasons is that hawkish politicians have increased in the opposition parties.

In the current political arena, the politician who excels the most in the enthusiasm to defend peace, and in the quantity and quality of efforts to accomplish it, in my opinion, is Nikai Toshihiro, Secretary-General of Liberal Democratic Party. The politicians of Komeito are in the same position with Nikai in that they are pacifists, and I think it is the biggest significance of the coalition goverment of LDP and Komeito.

During the 75 years since World War II ended, there was only one instance where Japanese Government did an aggressive act which was equal to creating a risk of war. It was in 2012, when Noda Yoshihiko of the Democratic Party of Japan(DPJ) was in power. On September 2012, Noda, the then Prime Minister, decided in a Cabinet meeting that the Senkaku Islands be nationalized. Noda accepted an advice by Ishihara Shintaro, then the governor of Tokyo Prefecture, ignored the opposition by the Chinese Government, took an aggressive attitude which seemed as if Japan were seeking an international conflict with China, and went ahead with the Cabinet decision of nationalizing the Senkaku islands. This made the Japan-China relations the worst since the establishment of diplomatic relations between the two countries in 1972. There was a risk of breakup of diplomatic relations, and military tension escalated. Noda engaged in an evil act that would cause a new Japan-China war.

Then, among the Cabinet members of Noda's administration, the one who strongly advocated the peace was Yamaguchi Tsuyoshi, then the State Minister for Foreign Affairs. Because Yamaguchi strongly opposed to the nationalization of the Senkaku islands, Noda did an outrageous act of dismissing him. Yamaguchi protested it and left DPJ. Being a former diplomat, he is a politician who has kept acting up to pacifism.

We Japanese people must not forget that Noda administration did the most dangerous act in the 75 years since World War II ended that threatened the peace. We must not repeat such a stupid act.

It proved the fact that the view of media personnel, that DPJ was more ardor for peace than LDP, were just a fixed and crooked notion. Immediately after that, DPJ lost the Lower House election and gave up the reins of government, though it was fought under the combination of single-seat constituencies and proportional representation which DPJ had adopted to realize the two-party system. Afterwards, the possibility for DPJ to come into power has been almost zero, and DPJ itself doesn't exist now. Therefore, Noda administration committed a great sin.

Under this difficult situation, many people began their efforts to remedy the critical circumstances between Japan and China. Among them, the most enthusiastic were the politicians of LDP such as Nikai Toshihiro, who had always acted up to pacifism, and the ones of Komeito, like Yamaguchi Natsuo, the head of the party, and Senator Nishida Makoto.

Especially, Yamaguchi acted quickly. On January 2013, Komeito sent a delegation to China, and Yamaguchi talked with Xi Jinping, Secretary-General of the Chinese Communist Party, and confirmed the policy of solving through dialogues.

And LDP followed it. Nikai, who has wide connections with Chinese officials, worked together with Komeito and sought the way of dialogue actively behind the scenes. Through various connections he had built, Nikai communicated to the high officials of China the fact that Japanese people hope for the friendship between Japan and China, and his intention that the relationship between the two countries should be considered from a long-term perspective. And Yamaguchi Tsuyoshi made his efforts as well. As a result of these efforts, the military crisis was avoided.

Among the members of Noda administration, the one who opposed to causing a confliction with China was Yamaguchi Tsuyoshi, then State Minister for Foreign Affairs. In front of Noda, Yamaguchi strongly supported the solution via dialogues, and crossed swords with Genba Koichiro, then Minister for Foreign Affairs.

Yamaguchi left DPJ, which had discarded pacifism, won two Lower House elections as an independent, and after entering the faction led by Nikai, a pacifist, joined LDP. Now, he works actively and widely as a high official of the party. Following is a testimony which he gave to me. Of course, I am responsible for the text.

"I haven't told it to anyone, but I did my best to prevent the Japan-China relations from getting the worst. I consulted with Mr. Nikai as well, and there was one thing which Mr. Nikai accomplished.

On May 2015, when I visited Beijing with 3,000 Japanese people, Chinese authorities discussed until the last minute and decided to hold a talk between Xi Jinping and Mr. Nikai. Through this talk, armed clashes and the crisis of war could be prevented. And I think the role of Mr. Nikai, who made it possible, was really big.

I was deeply afraid of the risk of armed clash that had arisen by the DPJ's messy handling of the Senkaku island in 2012. It was a real crisis in front of us.

(The previous day of the Cabinet decision of September 11th 2012, Yamaguchi, who was responsible for diplomacy with China as State

Minister for Foreign Affairs, visited the office of Prime Minister at the risk of his political life and talked with Noda man to man - Morita)

To Noda, I persisted, 'I would like you to postpone the tomorrow's Cabinet decision of nationalizing the Senkaku islands. Even if Tokyo Prefecture purchases them, it will take time and not possible until December, so I'm ready to visit Beijing everyday and discuss with them. Even if the policy of nationalization cannot be dropped, we should hold more discussions.

If the Cabinet decides the nationalization tomorrow, an endless number of anti-Japanese riots will occur in China. And the situation will get as tens of times, even hundreds of times, worse than you would imagine. There is even a risk of armed clash.

Even if we can avoid it, the relationship with China will freeze for seven or eight years. I sincerely ask you to postpone the Cabinet decision tomorrow and give me time to discuss with the officials in Beijing'.

Though, Prime Minister Noda said nothing. And when I left, I said to him, 'Is your silence a sign of approval?', but he still answered nothing.

This night, I got a call from Mr. Genba, which was rare, and crossed swords with him about the contents of tomorrow's Cabinet decision.

This is the story of the previous day of the Cabinet decision on September 11th 2012.

(As a result, the Cabinet decision was not changed, and afterwards, the situation get the worst as Yamaguchi Tsuyoshi had foretold - Morita)

At the press conference after the Cabinet meeting, I repeated loudly, in order for my voice to reach the high officials in Beijing, 'This issue shall be handled as a matter of the Ministry of Foreign Affairs. This must not be a military issue. This is a matter of the Ministry of Foreign Affairs, not of the Ministry of Defense'.

As a result, China dispatched just the ships of 'Coast Guard', not of the Navy, and Japan also dispatched coast guard, ensuring that unexpected incidents never led to a war.

Afterwards, I was really afraid of military conflicts, and there was a risk of it indeed.

Mr. Nikai would visit China on May 2015 with 3,000 people, and I would accompany him. So, on the previous month, I secretly visited Li Xiaolin, an old friend of mine and the chairperson of the Chinese People's Association for Friendship with Foreign Countries, with a secretary of Secretary-General, and asked her to arrange a talk between Mr. Nikai and Xi Jinping. She replied, 'it would be difficult but I'll do my best'".

This is the testimony Yamaguchi Tsuyoshi made to me. It reveals the tense situation of that time, and I am responsible for releasing it.

This testimony of Yamaguchi is a record of utmost historical importance.

It was LDP and Komeito that were committed to remedy the peaceful and friendly Japan-China relations which had been destroyed by the DPJ administration. And at the center of this effort was Nikai Toshihiro.

Not only since he was first elected to the Lower House, but since he was a member of the Wakayama Prefectural Assembly, Nikai has been a conservative politician who has acted up to pacifism. During the 37 years since he became a member of the Lower House in 1983, he has never ceased to make efforts for peace and Japanese people. Nikai Toshihiro is a statesman of peace who leads the politics of Japan.

As a pacifist, I regard any politician who makes efforts for peace as a soulmate. And Nikai Toshihiro is the leading person of pacifism in the political world of Japan. This is a reason why I trust and support him.

In 2020, the world faces a grave crisis. New coronavirus, which originates from Wuhan city of Hubei Province of China, has spread to many countries and terrified people around the world. And a movement to exclude Asian people, including people of China, Japan, and Korea, began to occur in some of European countries. If Covid-19 spreads further, the dangerous movement of excluding Asian people can get more serious. And though not general yet, a similar movement to exclude Chinese people can be seen in Japan, and contemptible attacks by anti-China activists against pro-China politicians have started.

These movements must not be tolerated.

For the peaceful life of humankind, tolerance and patience is absolutely necessary. Especially, politicians of major nations have to act up to them.

In order to realize the world peace, any nation must not shut away China. Japanese government should reinforce the efforts of international cooperation so that China can exist harmoniously with the countries around the world.

Of course, there is a possibility that movements to shut away China and the China bashing begin worldwide. Therefore, Japan have to make diplomatic efforts for China not to be excluded. For the world peace, one has to make Asia peaceful first. And Japan's role for it is really big.

The role of Nikai seems especially big in this situation of grave crisis. Japan needs to work hard to avoid shutting away China and to unify Asian countries.

I lay my hopes on Nikai Toshihiro. As a politician of peace and cooperation, he now faces the time to take inventory of his political life.

3. Nikai, a successor of Tanaka Kakuei who was a politician of peace and grassroots

I regard Tanaka Kakuei as a genius of politics.

In the period of parliamentary democracy after World War II, many excellent politicians appeared in the political world of Japan. And in my view, there were three politicians among them who could be called "genius". The first is Miki Bukichi, who accomplished the merger of the two conservative parties. The second is Tanaka Kakuei who accomplished the re-establishment of diplomatic relations between Japan and China, and the third is Nikai Toshihiro who is working actively now.

Tanaka was the political mentor of Nikai and paid attention to him from early on. After Nikai became a member of Diet and joined Tanaka faction, he studied with Tanaka directly. And Nikai learned from Tanaka a lot of the central conceptions of politics, such as ways of grasping things, a judgement of character, how to treat each other and the whole concept of political activities.

There are a lot of politicians who claim to be a political disciple of Tanaka. Many of them, though, have just worked near Tanaka, and imitate his outward political methods and words and deeds superficially. Therefore, some of them claiming to be a disciple of Tanaka, who was essentially a humble politician, tend to be arrogant and despise others, only to end up with being a third-class politician.

Nikai is totally different in this point; what he learned from Tanaka is the essence of Tanaka's politics, which can be called a political spirit. Nikai learned the origin of such things as the enormousness of Tanaka as a human, infinite kindness toward others, and the politics of serving people. He learned from Tanaka the essence of politics, inherited it personally, and has been practicing it in the arena of real politics for people.

Tanaka bequeathed a genius, Nikai Toshihiro, to the "post-Tanaka" political world of Japan. Nikai once spoke about the relationship with Tanaka and himself. It is a lecture which he gave in China on December 28th 2017. I quote the whole text of it here, hoping that the readers read it thoroughly.

"The Japan-China relations in the world—For the era of 'co-creating' of Japan and China" (A lecture at the Central Party School, December 28th 2017)

Dajia Hao!

I am Nikai Toshihiro, Secretary-General of Liberal Democratic Party of Japan.

I am honored to give a lecture at the Central Party School of the Chinese Communist Party.

I come to China for the first time in seven months in order to attend the seventh conference of the ruling parties of Japan and China, and have been in Fujian Province until yesterday, where President Xi Jinping spent 17 years, and the birthplace of Mr. Song Tao, the head of the International Liaison Department of the Chinese Communist Party.

I genuinely express my gratitude to Mr. He Yiting, executive vice president of the School, and the officials who gave me such a precious chance.

"You can chant Nembutsu a million times, but if you don't practice it, it will be meaningless".

"Determination and execution are important".

These are the words which Prime Minister Tanaka Kakuei, my "political mentor", told repeatedly.

This year, we celebrate the 45th anniversary of the re-establishment of diplomatic relations between Japan and China, and the new year is approaching now. In this memorial year, I would like to look back on the achievements of the leaders of Japan and China who made this historical decision.

On September 25th 1972, when Mr. Tanaka departed from Haneda Airport as the first Prime Minister who visited China, someone asked him why he would go to China. Mr. Tanaka answered "It is a flux of time". Even in the time of Cold War, when situations changes rapidly, Mr. Tanaka grasped the "flux of time" correctly, and looked ahead to not only the near future, but the Japan of 10 years and 100 years ahead.

Mr. Tanaka considered that a big decision was necessary to overcome all the problems in that age.

Meanwhile, in the Chinese side, which was receiving the Prime Minister of Japan for the first time, there were such great leaders as Chairman Mao Zedong and Premier Zhou Enlai, who had studied in Japan in his youth, who had the same strategical and long-term vision as Mr.

Tanaka.

However, vision was not enough to make a big achievement; courage to take risks and a political decision were necessary, because the voices that strongly opposed the re-establishment of diplomatic relations "echoed" in those days.

Yes, though I'm not sure whether it was an accident or a necessity of history, there were leaders who had clear-sightedness and courage in both Japan and China, in the same period of 45 years ago.

Under such great leaders, the relationship between the two countries began, and there is a episode.

On one night, Mr. Tanaka, who had been negotiating with Premier Zhou for three days, was suddenly asked to visit Zhongnanhai. There, Chairman Mao greeted him, and as they shook hands firmly and sat down, he said to Mr. Tanaka, "Have you finished the quarrel with Premier Zhou? A friendship emerges only after quarreling".

This word shows clearly that the top leaders of China held the broad perspective on the Japan-China relations. Afterwards, the negotiation went smoothly and the re-establishment of diplomatic relations was realized on September 29th.

This word by Chairman Mao pointed out the essence of the relationship between the two countries and shrewdly indicated the relationship not only then but afterwards.

We standing here today must not forget this political decision by the leaders of both Japan and China those days, and the great contributions of the forerunners who made efforts to "dig a well" in the process.

At the same time, when looking back on these 45 years, there was a history of various friendship and interactions.

In Yuyuantan Park, the most prominent cherry blossom viewing spot in Beijing, the Oyama cherry blossom which Mr. Tanaka donated as a memorial of the re-establishment of diplomatic relations blooms in spring even now.

In addition, a pair of beautiful ibises, which was at the verge of extinction in Japan, were donated to Japan in 1999.

Taking the opportunity afforded by it, artificial breeding was repeated, and the number of crested ibises in Japan has increased. And in turn, Japan has supported the protection of crested ibises in China. I would be really grateful if you kindly provide more crested ibises as a means of developing this cooperation further.

To inherit the determination and spirits of the forerunners for the friendship between Japan and China and pass down them to the next generation, I myself have planted trees, sowed seeds, and dug a well, holding Chairman Mao's words, "A friendship never emerges without quarreling" in my heart.

No matter how the situation is, Japan and China, the neighboring countries separated only by a strip of water, or "ichi-taisui", must not lose interactions and dialogues. This is my belief.

In 2000, when I was Minister of Transportation, I planned to form a delegation to China, with a goal of including 2,000 people after the number of that year. I talked to a lot of persons concerned and as a result, I could rally 4,000 people, the double of the goal.

When I told Tang Jiaxuan, Foreign Minister of China then, about this, he said, "We Chinese prefer the number 5 to 4".

I was surprised; do I have to rally 1,000 more people just before departing? Nevertheless, I talked to people again and could rally 5,200 people in total.

Then, though, I was told that the Great Hall of the People couldn't accommodate as many people as 5,000. I couldn't help but laugh bitterly, but in the end, of course, these 5,200 people were greeted warmly. Now, this episode is a fond memory.

Two years later, in 2002, celebrating the 30th anniversary of the re-establishment of diplomatic relations, I rallied 13,000 associates to plant 13,000 trees in Badaling section of the Great Wall, with one tree per each participant.

On October 2015, when I accompanied the NHK Symphony Orchestra's concert in Beijing, I visited Badaling for the first time in 13 years to see the trees we had planted. They had taken bold roots and grown up splendidly, with thick foliage in brilliant green. I was filled with joy. And here, I would like to extend my heartfelt gratitude to the people who have cared for them.

On May that year, when I visited China along with more than 3,000 cultural ambassadors as the exchange group of sightseeing and culture between Japan and China, President Xi taught me a saying, "Under a tree planted by an ancestor, people of the future generations take rests".

I was moved by President Xi's words that supported planting trees, which is my lifework, and when I saw the trees in Badaling, I remembered it vividly.

Thanks to the fact that our forerunners planted bold trees, that is, the re-establishment of diplomatic relations, and have kept bringing them up, even if hot and difficult issues arises between Japan and China, we can cool our heads under the shade of the trees and consider the future of Japan-China relations seriously. It is my belief that planting trees is the most prominent human activity that transcends worldly interests.

In 2011, when an unprecedent disaster hit Japan, many Chinese people extended their support to the Japanese people who were in need.

China sent forth the international rescue unit to Japan for the first time, and its 15 members arrived at Ofunato City of Iwate Prefecture and made efforts to search and rescue the survivors.

In addition, seeing prostrated children who had fallen victim to the disaster, Chinese government kindly invited 500 such children. And when the first 100 children visited China, I accompanied them.

Having departed from Sendai, which had been devastated by tsunami, we saw the blue sky and beautiful sea of Hainan island, and how smiles returned to the faces of the prostrated children. Seeing this, I keenly felt the importance of heart-to-heart interactions. The tender light streamed into their hearts.

In return, I proposed to invite five hundred Chinese children to Japan, and as a result of it, the interaction between Japanese and Chinese children was realized.

Even now, I receive letters from some of these Chinese children, who are now university students, and store them as precious evident of the goodwill and friendship between Japan and China.

And next year, we will commemorate the tenth anniversary of 2008 Sichuan earthquake. Both Japan and China have been hit by earthquakes often, so we can cooperate and tackle with a simple but difficult task, that is, protecting precious lives. I think this is a big pillar that will support the realization of a new relationship between Japan and China.

As such, through cooperation of Japan and China, I would like to keep supporting for national resilience worldwide where any life will not be lost by natural disasters.

During these several decades, China has achieved the outstanding economic growth and thousands of millions of middle-class citizens have emerged. I have visited China almost every year, seen the lives of Chinese people and the energy of cities developing everyday, and felt modest happiness on the faces of the people. I am really happy with it.

From now on, Japan and China should share goals, develop together, and, in reinforcing the perspective of "the Japan-China relations in the world", seek a possibility of the new and mutually complementary cooperation and collaboration of a higher-level.

An example of this is the issue of environment and energy saving.

Our generation has seen clean air and water, and green forests and rich soil has been lost around the world. There is nothing more heartbreaking than bequeathing such a planet to future generations.

Therefore, Japan and China should make use of their precious experiences and technologies, and cooperate and collaborate to deal with the environmental issues of the earth.

I believe that Japan and China can, or should, realize the "Ecological Civilization", on which President Xi is placing emphasis as well, and an eco-society which is kind to environment.

For example, the intellectual property.

As for the number of patent applications, China has been No.1 since 2011. If Japan and China cooperate to reinforce the protection of intellectual property, small companies of both country can invest on Japan and China and do business there. By doing so, the area of business cooperation of the two countries will extend more.

Another example is the area of sanitation.

I am aware of the movement of "Toilet Revolution" which, by President Xi's initiative, aims to popularize sanitary toilets in rural areas, and believe that high-quality and high-performance toilets made in Japan can contribute to this "Revolution".

Installing the advanced toilets made in Japan around the rural areas of China, and with these "model toilets" as a source, spreading a kind of "consciousness revolution" that "toilet is a peaceful sanctuary" all over China.

If it is realized, we Japanese will be able to support the development goal of "wonderful life" which President Xi proposed in the previous party congress.

How can we construct such a mutually complementary economic relationship that will progress to a higher stage? What kind of domestic reforms and bilateral cooperation are necessary to realize it? In order to discuss these long-term issues honestly and from a high perspective, I strongly hopes "Japan-China High-Level Economic Dialogue", which has been stopped for seven years, should be restarted as soon as possible.

Now I feel that this economical relationship between Japan and China has transcend the stage of "mutually beneficial" and reached the stage of "co-creation" in which we create the future together. Only when the cooperation between Japan and China extends beyond the two countries and contributes to the peace and prosperity of the world, will the Japan-China relations become appropriate in a new era, for Japan and China, which is the third and the second biggest economic power respectively, have the responsibility of contributing to Asia and the world.

Prime Minister Abe also says, ‘Japan and China cooperating and addressing this huge demand for infrastructure - this does not stop at the economical development of the two countries, but contribute greatly to the prosperity of the people in Asia”.

As agreed by the high officials of Japan and China, the business cooperation of Japan and China in third countries has the potential to establish a relationship where, with Japan, China, and ASEAN countries cooperating, one more “win” can be added to the win-win relationship between Japan and China.

Furthermore, companies of Japan and China will cooperate and make efforts in South-East Asia. It might not be difficult to imagine.

Or, the cooperation for disaster prevention.

We celebrated the first “World Tsunami Awareness Day” last year, and on November I held the “World Tsunami Awareness Day Summit” by high school students and invited about 250 students from 29 countries. From China, 60 students participated.

Enhancing children’s awareness for disaster prevention should lead to the disaster reduction in the future. If Japan and China cooperate to spread such an initiative all over the world, it will lead to the international cooperation of global scale with Japan China as its leader.

Tsunamis in Indonesia, typhoons in Philippines, and earthquakes in Nepal. In Asia, where natural disasters frequently occur, Japan and China should cooperate to open the world’s eyes to disaster-prevention and enlarge the circle for national resilience around the world.

Compared to the time of the re-establishment of diplomatic relations, it is true that the channel between Japan and China has narrowed. As many young politicians, scholars, journalist, artists, and scientists as possible, who will lead the future, should visit each country and interact each other. The relationship between countries is ultimately the relationship between people. If there isn't a heart-to-heart trust, we can never develop together. If there is a person for whom one is willing to do everything or make efforts, the impression on the country to which he belongs will change drastically.

I send forth young lawmakers of Japan to China every year. Without future leaders of Japan and China crossing swords face-to-face and sometimes quarreling, the true mutual trust will never emerge.

Chairman Mao taught us it 45 years ago. We might have different opinions, and sometimes quarrel. As you see in the current situation around East China Sea, we, neighbors who cannot move to other places, may want to outdo the other and bring difficult situations.

However, as I said at the first, we must not stop interactions and dialogues between Japan and China. A relationship where we can talk anytime is necessary.

I sincerely hope that the students of the Central Party School who lead the future of China come to Japan and interact with young politicians. We welcome you from our heart.

In 2018, we will celebrate the 40th anniversary of signing the Japan-China Peace and Amity Treaty, and I propose to invite the students of the School every year.

There is a teaching in "Analects", 'If one doesn't have a long-term perspective, he will meet a problem in the near future".

It means that if one doesn't have a long-term perspective, he cannot overcome the problem in front of him. 45 years ago, the great leaders of Japan and China made a broad political decision, and it made the re-establishment of diplomatic relations between the two countries possible.

When one thinks of the difficulties which those leaders overcame, we politicians of both countries should learn the courage, decisiveness, and faculty of them.

Now is the time to establish the future vision for eternal peace greater than that of those days, because there are powerful leaders in both countries now.

Let us remember the words of Mr. Tanaka 45 years ago, and catch this “flux of time”.

Last month, the summit meeting between Prime Minister Abe and President Xi was held, and Mr. Abe described it by saying, “President Xi said that this talk was a beginning of the new Japan-China relations. I totally agree with it”. And Mr. Abe added, “I would like to hold the summit meeting between Japan, China, and South Korea and invite Premier Li Keqiang. In addition, I will visit China at an appropriate time next year, and would like President Xi to visit Japan as soon as possible. Through the communications between high officials, I would like to push up the Japan-China relations to a new phase”.

Let the both leaders talk about the future of the Japan-China relations honestly. As in the saying, ‘People come first, and nation next’, one should pursue politics for people. Those who can promise it are such strong leaders as Prime Minister Abe and President Xi.

In the 19th Party Congress, President Xi also said, “we will never struggle for hegemony forever”. I would like to praise this word.

Both Japan and China value “Jin(human-heartedness)” and “Toku(virtue)”, so, in the new age of new Japan-China relations, let us walk on the “path of King”.

Both Japan and China have to develop the “co-creation” relationship further and pursue the permanent peace of the world.

Japan and China, which have gotten off to a new start, need a long-term vision which acts as a guidepost for the future. And in terms of spaces, a broad perspective to “consider the future” in the world is necessary.

I would like to entrust the will of forerunners, who had made an effort to "dig a well", to the current leaders and those present here who will be responsible for the future. And I pledge to keep working for it. I would like to thank you all for listening so attentively."

Reading it, how do you feel? It may be a long quotation, but I think it is a historical speech by Nikai Toshihiro.

The Central Party School is an institution that trains up the future high officials of CCP and a place where those future leaders of a superpower, China, gather together. And in his speech, Nikai described this picture, at the same time looking back on the Japan-China relations in a historical perspective. He explained to the students the achievements of the past leaders such as Tanaka Kakuei, Mao Zedong, Zhou Enlai, who achieved the re-establishment of diplomatic relations between Japan and China, and, to the people of both Japan and China as well, why Japan and China should encourage amicable relations.

On May 2017, when Nikai made this speech, the first "One Belt, One Road Initiative Forum", which was based on one of the major policies of "One Belt, One Road Initiative" by Xi Jinping, was held. For President Xi, it was an international forum of tremendous importance where he would declare the future of China to the world.

Though, the international community, especially Western countries, regarded it as a means of China to pursue hegemonism, and the leaders of major countries didn't participate. Japan also followed America and made it clear that Prime Minister would not participate. Among the leaders of major countries, only President Putin of Russia and Prime Minister Gentiloni of Italy attended at the forum.

Though Japan had expressed its non-attendance, Chinese government sent a letter of invitation to Nikai. Receiving the letter, Nikai instantly expressed his attendance and participated in the forum. Hayashi Motoo, who has always been close to him, testified about the situation of those days.

"Japan and America had expressed their non-attendance. But when Mr. Nikai received the letter of invitation from Chinese government, he said, 'we cannot decline this invitation from our neighbor' and instantly decided to visit China.

The office of Prime Minister, which had followed America and declared Japan would not participate in the forum, implied that Secretary-General Nikai should not visit China if possible. There was also opinions that it would be better for Mr. Nikai not to visit China at this time. Mr. Nikai, though, decided to participate with a determination; it was "Nikai Mission" by Mr. Nikai himself.

Then, business associations expressed their intention to attend at the forum, and Ministry of Economy, Trade and Industry also expressed their intention to send forth the deputy minister. Furthermore, the office of Prime Minister, which had implied Mr. Nikai should not visit China, asked him to take a secretary of Prime Minister with him. Mr. Nikai expressed his attitude that those who wanted to visit China could accompany him. As a result, though Prime Minister did not participate in the forum, many people did so with Mr. Nikai".

This testimony by Hayashi describes well the atmosphere then. The decision by Nikai resulted in supporting Chinese government and Xi Jinping.

Therefore, though Nikai is not the head of the state, Xi treated him so, talking with him separately; it was made possible because Nikai had continued his diplomatic activities.

Nikai's speech in the Central Party School referred to not only various challenges of Japan and China, but also realistic issues. And he made a lot of concrete recommendations.

Nikai held a high ideal, and at the same time told about down-to-earth realities carefully. This is his true value; he not only spoke of how to cope with the current challenges of Japan and China, but explained clearly how the two countries should go ahead.

In that sense, it seems to me that his speech was historical one from the perspective of how to construct the Japan-China relations.

4. Nikai Toshihiro, an inheritor of Wakayama Spirit and Spirit of Independence of Minakata Kumagusu

What Nikai Toshihiro and Minakata Kumagusu share

About 30 years ago, I received an invitation from the supporters' group of Nikai and landed at Nanki Shirahama Airport. Though I had known Nanki province is a wonderful area, I was not sure where to visit first as there are too many alluring places there. So, I asked Nikai directly, and he instantly answered "Minakata Kumagusu". I found that Minakata was the most important person to him.

I was guided to a facility in which documents on Minakata were stored. The two-storied building was old and seemed to me too simple to research that great genius of world level.

The building was filled with documents and one had to walk sideways. The director who greeted me was a top scholar. He explained to me the achievements of Minakata for several hours and provided me with a lot of documents. Afterwards, I declined any other works for a full month to read all those documents and study the achievements of Minakata. As a result, I found that he was a great person who was comparable with God and Buddha.

After this studying, I learned that the scholars whom I had regarded as "brilliant" or "genius" were a nobody compared to Minakata. It was as if the sun rose and the stars which had been shining in the dark sky disappeared suddenly.

Minakata Kumagusu was a great genius who transcended any

scholars of Japan from whom I learned.

What I learned from studying Minnakata was that while his academic achievements were enormous, he was grand and pure, and had a spirit of independence that never gave in to authority.

Then, I felt as if I touched the nature of Nikai Toshihiro. Nikai is a genius of politics, grand in personality, and had a pure heart and a spirit of independence. I thought he and Minakata were the same in their nature.

Afterwards, I have interacted with Nikai for more than 30 years. During this period, the image of Nikai's personality which emerged when I studied Minakata hasn't changed a bit, and I have been feeling that Nikai is the reincarnation of Minakata.

I have once visited the memorial building of Minakata in Nanki city, which was constructed after my first visit to Nanki province. It is a great facility.

Soon after my visit to Nanki, I went to Kinokawa city and studied about Hanaoka Seisyu. During these 30 years, I have visited the grave of Hanaoka three times, and each time Nakamura Shinji, who is the mayor of the city and my friend, guided and tended me. I read a lot of documents about Hanaoka as well. As a result, I have been feeling the existence of a mind similar to Wakayama Spirit, "One must serve for the world and others", which has been inherited from Hanaoka and Minakata to Nikai.

The basis of this Wakayama Spirit is the grand environment of Wakayama. First, it is a spirit of breadth, generousness, and harmony which arise from the great landscape of Kii Peninsula and the Pacific Ocean. Secondly, it is a strong spirit of independence by which people live up to Wakayama Spirit.

What I have been feeling during the 30 years of interactions with Nikai is the greatness and breadth of Nikai's personality, and his kindness and humanity that encompass everyone. To me, it seems to relate with the environment and culture unique to Kii Peninsula.

The environment of Kisyu and the character of Wakayama people

In all countries, it has been pointed out that the environment in which one grows up affects him in some ways. The word " 風土 (fuudo, or environment)" has been used to describe the climate, geography, geology, and landscape of this area collectively. In ancient Japan, it was called " ふど (fudo)", and the central government ordered the editing of the ' 風土記 (Record of Fudo)' in Nara era(713).

In the West, Ionian scholars in ancient Greece discarded mythological view of world and tried to discuss the human society and other ethnic distinctions by understanding nature through the 4 elements of soil, water, air, and fire. As its successor, Aristotle referred to the relationship between environment and political system in his 'Politics' and pointed out that environment affects the character formation.

Afterwards, many attempts were made to clarify the relationship between nature and human. For example, Montesquieu, one of the forerunners of Renaissance, said that the influence of environment is crucial. And in Japan, ' 風土 '(1953) by Watsuji Teturo, a philosopher, is widely known as an unique essay on environment.

Anyway, people have strongly felt in the flux of history that the environment in which one grows up affects his character formation and way of thinking.

Gobou city of Wakayama Prefecture, where Nikai Toshihiro grew up, locates on the western side of Kii Peninsula and is blessed with a warm climate as well as agriculture products and seafoods. Meanwhile, it has experienced a lot of hardships in which one cannot help but keenly sense the historically harsh power of nature.

The most notable person born in Kisyu Wakayama is Minakata Kumagusu. When comparing him and Nikai, one will be surprised with their similarity. Since Minakata was not a politician, when discussing about Nikai, one has rarely considered them on the same plane, but it seems to me that they are master and pupil who share the same spirit.

Minakata Kumagusu, the "great intellectual figure" whom today's youngsters respect the most

Recently, a TV program reported the result of a questionnaire which had been conducted on the students of Tokyo University.

The question was "Who is your most respected historical figure in Japan?", and the "greatest figure in Japanese history" whom they respected was Minakata Kumagusu. The second is Oda Nobunaga, and such warlords as Tokugawa Yeyasu and Toyotomi Hideyosi followed.

Minakata Kumagusu was a genius who was known to limited persons.

Minakata was born in 1867 in Wakayama Prefecture and passed away in 1941 at 74. He was a natural historian and made achievements in the field of biology and folklore studies. And especially as a biologist, he was engaged in the study of Myxomycete and collected mushrooms, algae, moss, high plants, insects and even small animals on his own to study them. And in the process to systematize them, he established the concept of ecology for the first time in Japan.

After coming to Tokyo from Wakayama, he entered Kyoritsu School of Kanda (currently Kaisei High school) and the preparatory school for Tokyo University (the predecessor of the former National First Upper Secondary School, currently Tokyo University). His preparatory school classmates included such figures as Natsume Soseki, Masaoka Shiki, Akiyama Saneyuki, Yamada Bimyo, and Honda Kotaro. Afterwards he went to U.S. then to England and studied in British Museum. His period of studying abroad was as long as 14 years, and he wrote a lot of theses and books.

One of well-known episodes of Minakata is that he got attention by presenting a thesis written in English in the prestigious 'Nature' in 1893. Afterwards, 51 theses of him were published in 'Nature' in his lifetime, and it is said to be the record number of theses by a single author published in the journal. He was called a "walking encyclopedia" for his depth of knowledge.

Minakata's academic interest began with natural science such as biology, but it did not stop at it; he studied the folklore, legendary, and religion in Japan, and has been known as a forerunner of folklore study in Japan with his wide knowledge. Yanagida Kunio, who had close interactions with Minakata, remembered him as an "utmost limit of the potentials of Japanese".

Kisyu people and Minakata Kumagusu

As such, Minakata is worshiped by the people of Kisyu Wakayama as a "great intellectual figure", and "Minakata Kumagusu Museum" has been constructed in Nishimuro District of Shirahama Town in Wakayama Prefecture to show his achievements. Precious documents that represent his achievements are displayed and the visitor can see "Myxomycete" which Minakata discovered through a microscope. The main building was opened in 1965 and a lot of documents by Minakata are stored in it. The museum is 20-minute drive from Nanki Shirahama Airport, and the elegant new wing of two-storied reinforced-concrete building was opened in 2017. It's landscape, which looks down Tanabe Bay, is beautiful, and the museum is one of the precious sightseeing assets of Nanki Shirahama.

To me, the fact that Wakayama people constructed a facility which honors Minakata seems to show how profoundly they worship and take pride in Minakata Kumagusu. And a sentence which is carved in the "monument of constructing Minakata Museum", which stands on the garden of the museum, shows the feeling of Wakayama people towards Minakata: "We, the people of Wakayama prefecture, in order to pass down the honor of intimacy with Minakata and his great achievements for eternity, have chosen this beautiful place which is near Kamijima island, where the Emperor has visited, ... and on March 1965, this museum was completed and we made it the memorial of eternity along with this monument".

In addition to this museum, there is "Minakata Kumagusu Archives" in Tanabe city of Wakayama Prefecture. It places next to the old home of Minakata, where he had lived for 37 years since 1904, and stores the books and various documents of him. The people of Wakayama Prefecture not only maintain the achievements of Minakata as a building, but regularly hold "Minakata Kumagusu Seminar" and "Study Sessions about Kumagusu" to pass down the spirit of this local great figure.

What Nikai Toshihiro, a politician, and Minakata Kumagusu, a scholar, have in common

Both Nikai Toshihiro and Minakata Kumagusu are holder of a strong spirit of independence and the Wakayama spirit. Nikai lives in the world of politics, while Minakata lived in the academic world, and their world seems totally different on the surface. Though, I couldn't help but feel that these two figures born in Wakayama have a lot in common. In my view, if one compares Nikai to a historic figure, it is Minakata who resembles him the most. In other words, Nikai is a Minakata Kumagusu in the world of politics.

First of all, they share the spirit of independence at the bottme of their way of life. Minakata never succumbed to authority and pursued his intellectual interests on the basis of his academic creed. He could have easily got an authoritative status with his world-class academic achievements, but he declined the professorship.

Nikai, too, has survived in the world of politics with a spirit of independence. While most politicians seek to be Prime Minister, the most alluring position in the country, Nikai has chosen a different path. He has never had an ambition to be No.1, but regardless of his position lived up to the realization of "a politics for the world and people".

In addition, they are similar in that their view is not limited to Japan only. Minakata was so enlightened as to present his own academic achievement in international stages, and in a sense his achievements have been valued more highly overseas than in Japan.

Nikai, too, has been engaged in "personal diplomacy" and "diplomacy as a lawmaker", both of which not so many Japanese politicians do.

Nikai tends to be seen as a domestic politician because he has dealt with various challenges within Japan, but it is far from the truth. In this point, Japanese media people have to reflect on themselves. They see Nikai's words and deeds and pursue just the surface of his domestic politics, but it is a mistake. I say again that Nikai is not just a domestic politician; he has the same international view with that of Kumagusu and continued his lawmakers-initiated diplomatic activities on his own.

These are the actual feelings of mine, who visited abroad and interviewed with many people about lawmakers-initiated diplomatic activities of Nikai. I have strongly felt how high officials of China, Korea, and Asian countries trust and respect him, and heard with my own ears how they value Nikai as the most trustful friend. Nikai is a true cosmopolitan and the pioneer of lawmakers-initiated diplomatic activities.

In addition, as another common point of Kumagusu and Nikai, one can point out the breadth of them which does not pay attention to how others would evaluate them. Before Kumagusu, only 36 species of Myxomycete had been discovered and recorded, and he added a lot of new species to them. However, he neither recorded nor reported them as his own discovery. In the academic world, researchers after Kumagusu reported them in their theses, and Kumagusu hasn't been evaluated academically. Though, his achievements haven't been denied, and efforts have been continued to confirm them from his notes and diaries. Minakata Kumagusu is really a great figure.

It applies to Nikai as well. His political achievements are too numerous to list here, but he never speaks loud of his own achievements. In the first place, Nikai does not say a lot about himself. Although his skillful speeches allure people and he is eloquent enough not to bore others in conversations, he never boasts about his political achievements. Sometimes it seems that he suffers a loss as a politician, to whom achievement is everything, but he never cares for it.

Minaka and Nikai are also alike in that they strongly oppose to and fight against unfair discrimination.

In British Museum, the main research place of Minakata when he was studying in England, he was tossed a racist comment by a visitor because he was Asian. Kumagusu faced up to it firmly and gave him a head-butt in front of a lot of witnesses, banned entrance to the Museum for three months. Similar incident occured a year later, so he was banned entrance permanently, but British people who had valued his talent submitted a petition so that he was permitted to enter the Museum again.

Nikai Toshihiro, who is always polite and holds an attitude of a gentleman, has sternly addressed unfair discrimination which exist in the world even now. This attitude is based on a strong belief which he has held since his childhood. When he was a student of Gobou junior high school, he participated in a speech contest held by an extra-government organization and made an admirable speech quoting ‘Hakai (The Broken Commandment)’ by Shimazaki Toson.

Nikai, who developed a firm belief in his childhood that he would never forgive unfair discrimination, has lived up to this belief. On December 9th 2016, “Act for Eliminating Buraku Discrimination” passed Upper House plenary session and was enacted. This law was made possible by the all-out efforts by Nikai and others, and finally enacted through lawmaker-initiated legislation. Yamaguchi Tsuyoshi, who made efforts for this law in the Diet, is a disciple and ally of Nikai. It is significant that the law was created through the efforts of such people as Nikai and Yamaguchi.

“Eliminating Buraku discrimination” is an ardent wish of the people of Wakayama, who has suffered from discrimination for a long time. And it has been a central political challenge for Nikai, a politician from Wakayama Prefecture.

Nikai Toshihiro is a genuine politician of democracy.

Nikai Toshihiro is a statesman who represents the people of Japan.

Nikai is an inheritor of the spirit of the Seventeen-article constitution,

"Harmony is important", and that of the Oath in Five Articles, "Deliberative assemblies shall be widely established and all matters decided by open discussion", and a genuine democrat who defends liberty, equality, and basic human rights to the end. He is the "treasure of the people of Japan", as well as the treasure of the people of Wakayama Prefecture.

5. Nikai Toshihiro was "a child prodigy" in his childhood and an excellent leader in his high school days

Nikai Toshihiro grew up in Gobo city of Wakayama Prefecture and entered Hidaka high school. Hidaka high school was established in 1914 and has been a central school of the Hidaka area of Wakayama Prefecture. Since the days of the former Hidaka junior high school, it motto has been "Be a good student and a good athlete" and "Be simple and sturdy", and is widely known for developing a character with a harmony of intellect, virtue, and body.

From the fiscal year 2016 to 2020, Hidaka high school was designated as Super Global High school (SGH) by Ministry of Education, Culture, Sports, Science and Technology. And when the "2018 High school Student Summit of 'World Tsunami Awareness Day'" was held in Wakayama Prefecture in 2018, the students of Hidaka high school presented a research product "Raising Awareness of Disaster prevention - Let's make our Networks" from "the class of pursuing SGH challenges", and was highly evaluated. At the same time, the host and chairperson of the overall conference of this summit were the students of Hidaka High school. Nikai Toshihiro, who was a graduate of this school, made all-out efforts to realize the global event of the "World Tsunami Awareness Day", and his junior fellows participated actively in it.

It was in 2018 that I was requested to write the biography of Nikai from the leaders and secretaries of Nikai Group. And when I started to do research, I could find almost no one who knew Nikai's childhood. However, I was able to hear the testimonies from two persons. One told me, "Mr. Nikai was a brilliant boy and some called him 'a child prodigy'". And the other testified, "When Mr. Nikai was a junior high and high school student, he was an outstanding leader. He was clearly different from other boys". As such, Nikai was an excellent boy, though he rarely speaks of his childhood.

One time, during a conversation with him, I heard from him a episode of his high school days. Nikai, who usually speaks not much about himself, recalled it pleasantly.

In spring of 1956, when he was a student of Hidaka high school, the school was chosen to participate in the National High School Baseball Invitational Tournament (Koushien Baseball Championship) of this year. Originally, Hidaka was an elite high school, and its baseball team was not so strong. In Wakayama Prefecture, where there were many schools known for their baseball team, such as the former Wakayama junior high school, it was extraordinarily difficult to proceed to Koshien, and it was the first time Hidaka high school participated in the Tournament.

Nikai was the president of student union then. Hidaka high school was a school of tradition where students constructed their school life independently, so Nikai had to plan how to do cheering in Koshien. He decided not to rely on the teachers, and the students took initiative to form a cheering group to support the baseball team.

At that time, Nikai was not sure what to do. There wasn't an active cheering group as in other schools which participated in Koshien Tournament frequently, and Hidaka high school didn't have a brass band team needed to do cheering in Koshien.

Then, what Nikai did first was to do research on how to do cheering in a baseball match. In those days, students baseball matches, especially those by Tokyo Six Universities, were popular. Thus, he searched for a person who had graduated from one of these Six Universities and returned to Wakayama to learn the atmosphere and ways of cheering.

Nikai's idea was appropriate, but he could not find a graduate of Tokyo Six Universities. In spite of this, it was an excellent idea for a high school student, in that he tried to collect appropriate information in the first.

Then, Nikai came up with an idea which no one would expect; if there is not a cheering group, one can ask schoolgirls to line up and do cheering. It is what one would call "cheerleaders" now. In those days, there were no schoolgirls cheerleaders in high school baseball tournaments. Hearing Nikai's proposal, the schoolgirls all shrank away, saying, "We can't do that. It is a shame, and if we do such a thing, we cannot get married". But Nikai persuaded them, saying, "It is okay, and you can marry. In case of need, I will find husbands for you". Remembering this episode, Nikai smiled bitterly and said, "Of course, it was reckless, but afterwards, they all married, so I didn't have to find husbands for them".

The first game of Hidaka high school was the first match of the first day of the Tournament. The opponent was Namekawa high school of Toyama Prefecture, the representative of Hokuriku Area. The game was really close, and in the end, a rematch was declared with the score of 1-1. It would be held the next day. No one could expect it and they were not prepared, of course.

In this unexpected situation, Nikai asked the students that those who had relatives in Kyoto, Osaka, and Kobe area stayed there and came to Koshien the next day, and if not, returned to Wakayama and came back to Koshien the next morning. It is a surprising that a high school student could deal with such a sudden situation calmly. In the first place, it would be a responsibility of teachers and adult around them.

And the rematch on the next day hadn't been scheduled originally. The number of the cheering group was fewer than the previous day. Nikai, the president of the student union, thought it was a problem, and "Musical instruments are necessary, but our school doesn't have any. Ah, if we don't have a brass band, we can borrow it from another school along with the players".

Thus, he asked a school which was waiting for the second match of the day, saying, "I would like you to cheer up our school with your brass band. It would be a rehearsal for the second match. In return, we will cheer you up in the second match". Perhaps as a result of Nikai's eagerness, the brass band of the school did cheering for Hidaka high school.

As a result, Hidaka high school won the rematch with the score of 2-0. Though it lost in the second match, the first participation in the Koshien Tournament was successful thanks to the idea and excellent leadership of Nikai.

Though Nikai seldom boasts about himself, he told me this episode as a pleasant reminiscence of his youth. I think this story has been known to almost no one.

Nikai himself told this story casually, but it was his character that when he was as young as a high school student, he collected appropriate information to deal with a situation, thought what to do if lacked necessary things, came up with how to deal with a sudden incident, and did all these things naturally. A person who knew those days said, "Mr. Nikai was a genius".

To me, such a talent seems a natural gift, for ordinary high school students cannot do such things. And this kind of leadership was fully used when Nikai grew up and acted as a politician.

6. Nikai's resolution as the Secretary-General in his resent words

In his "New Year's greeting" in 2020 ('Jiyu-Minsyu' 2020 New Year Edition), Secretary-General Nikai emphasized the importance of being "humble".

"Last year, we faced great disasters nationwide, such as Northern-Kyusyu Heavy Rainstorm on August and the Typhoon No.15(Faxai) and No.16(Peipah). Nothing is more important than speed in order to complete the restoration and reconstruction of the affected areas as soon as possible. And in the regular Diet session, it is absolutely necessary to quickly pass "the fiscal year Reiwa 1 supplementary budget bill" and "the fiscal year Reiwa 2 budget bill" which include the provision for restoration and reconstruction, avoidance of the downward risk of the economy, and investment for the future.

Recently, natural disasters have occurred frequently which exceed the estimations made heretofore, so we will drive disaster-prevention, disaster-reduction, and national resilience.

The Abe Cabinet has marked its 8th year. During this period, GDP has increased by 65 trillion yen, the profit of companies by 35 trillion yen, the national and local tax revenues by 28 trillion yen, and the number of workers by three million and eighty-four thousand. In addition, there has been the reinforcement of Japan-U.S. alliance and the passage of the Legislation for Peace and Security, and liberty, democracy, basic human rights, and reign of law have been strengthened steadily.

As such, the Cabinet has been highly evaluated both nationally and internationally, but it is important to keep "humbleness" and "politeness". One has to learn what he should learn humbly and correct what he should correct rightly. One must keep these attitudes in his hearts to advance the politics.

Thanks to the support by the people and the members and friends of the party, we could do well in the last year's nationwide local elections and Upper House elections. And this year, we will mobilize the collective effort of the party to win the elections of every level. As a conclusion of my New Year greeting, I truly hope the health and happiness of the people and the members and friends of the party".

This "New Year's greeting" by Nikai was published in the 2020 New Year

Edition of 'Jiyu-Minsyu', the official paper of Liberal Democratic Party, along with the greeting by Abe Shinzo, the President of the party. Though it was a contribution to the official paper, the author was the Secretary-General of the party, so it can be regarded as a greeting to the entire nationals.

In the greeting, what Nikai emphasized the most was "to learn humbly" and "to do politics politely". In this short greeting, one can read the political attitude of Nikai.

First, the well-balanced sense of him. Japan and the world now face frequent natural disasters caused by the climate change, and Nikai made a suggestion about how to deal with them. As well as this, he emphasized the importance of "disaster-prevention, disaster-reduction, and national resilience", listed the policies realized by the Cabinet, and referred to not only domestic politics but diplomacy.

Here I repeat that it is significant that Nikai referred to the importance of being "humble" and "polite"; leading politicians have a responsibility to achieve accountability to the people.

Distrust in politics and political apathy of young people, both of which are apparent these days, are mainly due to the fact that politicians haven't achieved this kind of accountability. The resolution of Nikai that "one has to correct what he should correct" clearly shows his political attitude.

In the interviews with reporters of newspapers, magazines, and TV programs, Nikai always emphasizes the importance of peace. For example, he told in an interview published in March 2018 Edition of 'Gekkan Nihon (Monthly Japan)';

> "Japan cannot and must not wage a war. What Japan can do is to keep peace-oriented diplomacy.
>
> There is no other way than that. Japan should keep a humble attitude further, and deploy the peace-oriented diplomacy...

(Answering to the question about Japan-Korea relations) Japan and Korea is the closest neighbors both historically and geographically. If it were a distant country placed in the opposite side of the earth, we could overcome the difficulties by some patience. But Korea is our neighbor, so we have to be friendly with them".

From these concise words, one can see that Nikai Tosihiro is a total pacifist and has made efforts for the world peace. I repeat again that defending peace is the principal task of politics. To me, the scale to evaluate politicians is their approach to the realization of peace. A politician who lacks interest in defending peace or enthusiasm for it doesn't have the quality of a leading statesman.

Nikai Toshihiro is a "be all action and no talk" type of politician, and a man of action. To borrow the words of Confucius, he is a politician of "sturdiness and quietness are one's virtue" type. He never decorates himself with unnecessary euphuism and flatter others.

However, when it comes to "peace", Nikai, as in the interview quoted above, clearly preaches the importance of "peace diplomacy" with plain words so that anyone can understand.

Chapter 2

Nikai Toshihiro is the best and brightest No.2 statesman who surpasses No.1 politicians

1. A powerful "No.2"

Nikai Toshihiro is truly a "politician of harmony". He has never engaged in political wars carelessly, but acted actively in the center of political world, always focusing on the harmony with others, and considering what is important in politics and what action is beneficial to the people. Such an attitude doesn't stop at just managing the domestic politics, but as for the Diet members-initiated diplomatic activities as well, which is his lifework as a politician, he always focuses on the situation of counterparts, and engages in the diplomatic activities in the way that the counterpart can get an advantage from them as well.

A man who knows Nikai in his youth said, "Since he was young, his goal has been to be the Secretary-General of LDP, the second highest position in the world of politics". And Nikai has fulfilled this goal, become the first Secretary-General who has been in this position for a fourth consecutive term, his total tenure in office as Secretary-General surpassed that of Tanaka Kakuei, and recorded the longest on September 2020.

According to an old acquaintance of him, since he embarked on the career of a politician, Nikai hasn't aspired to be a Prime Minister, the most powerful position in Japan. I, too, think that he has lived his political life thinking that Secretary-General of LDP is his final goal; Nikai knows himself very well, and has felt the emptiness of struggling for the position of No.1. And intelligence and patience made it possible. By devoting his attention to act as No.2, he has lived up to the reason and belief as a politician and served purely for the people.

In order to be a Prime Minister, one has to be not only a Diet member but also the President of LDP. And in order to be the President of LDP, he has to win the election. To be No.1, it is imperative that he win the fierce political struggles. Nikai is a man of harmony, so does not like fierce struggles for power. It is because he knows how such struggles are unproductive and meaningless.

My understanding is that Nikai has chosen the path to "No.2" for that reason. I think he knows that even if he is No.2, he can do more great works than "No.1"; he has known the lives of "No.2" figures such as Zhuge Kongming and Katsu Kaisyu from his early days.

If one aspires to be the top person, he sometimes has to sacrifice his ideal. But "No.2"s can stick to his ideal. I think that by devoting his entire attention to being a "No.2", Nikai has lived up to his belief and ideal as a politician.

When one looks back on the history, powerful "No.2" figures sometimes have acted more actively than "No.1" figures and created the history of human societies. The accomplishments of such great "No.2" figures as Zhuge Kongming, Katsu Kaisyu, Suzuki Kantaro, and Miki Bukichi surpassed those of "No.1" figures. Nikai is a powerful politician listed in this genealogy.

From this "No.2" viewpoint, which has rarely been referred to when one speaks about politicians, I would like to explain the true image of Nikai as a politician.

2. Powerful No.2 figures surpass inferior No.1 persons and make the history—Nikai Tosihiro is "No.2" type politician like Zhuge Kongming and Katsu Kaisyu

When a historical shift occurs, powerful "No.2" figures often emerge who is as great as, or greater than, "No.1" persons. In a period like this, such a "No.2" figure is by no means merely a backseat player, but moves the era and create a new history as a main character.

One of these "No.2" politicians who acted actively enough to be recorded in the history was Zhuge Kongming, the main character of 'Romance of the Three Kingdoms'. Though he was highly competent, he never aspired to be the top figure. Though "Three visits to the cottage" by Liu Bei Xuande, Zhuge Kongming became his military advisor and acted as "No.2". It is because Zhuge Kongming didn't have any personal feeling, but always grasped things from a higher viewpoint and showed the direction which "No.1" persons should pursue that he has kept impressing the future generations. It is excellent "No.2" figures that act as a compass for a nation to proceed forward rightly.

In Japan, the representative "No.2" in the last days of Edo era was Katsu Kaisyu. In those chaotic times, he played a great role. There is never "if" in the history, but if Katsu Kaisyu hadn't appeared, the modernization of Japan would be impossible and even the existence of Japan could be at risk.

Japan faced a crisis in the last days of World War II as well.

During this period, as well as during the period of merger of the conservative parties, Suzuki Kantaro and Miki Bukichi emerged as powerful "No.2" figures. And Nikai Tosihiro is a successor of them. In my view, the "three greatest No.2 figures" after World War II are Suzuki, Miki, and Nikai.

Nikai's way of life is similar to that of Katsu Kaisyu, Suzuki Kantaro, and Miki Bukichi. They are all the powerful "No.2" politicians who represents Japan.

They were all pacifists and had a heart of benevolence. While keeping confidential relationship with the top figures, they were courageous enough to present candid advice about them. "Call what is right right, and wrong wrong"—they share their ideal to stick to straight way of life. They all took pride in themselves and lived up to it.

In the next section, I will overview how the great "No.2" figures in history lived their lives.

3. Zhuge Liang—A gifted military advisor who supported Liu Bei to the end

I was born in 1932 and entered an elementary school on April 1939. In those days, I already read books for small boys, and among them was 'Romance of the Three Kingdoms', which was loved by both adults and children alike.

The main character of the story is Zhuge Kongming. He was popular among Japanese people then, and many of its reader hoped to live like him.

What kind of person was Zhuge Kongming (181-234)? Here I quote the article on him from "The World Encyclopedia" of Heibon-Sha (the author of the article is Kawakatsu Yoshio).

"Zhuge Kongming was a chancellor of Shu during the Three Kingdoms period and thought as a representative loyal subject. His autonym was Liang, and he is also known as Zhuge Liang, but his courtesy name, Kongming, is more popular. He was born in Langya Commandery (present-day Yishui, Shandong Province), but as his father died when he was still young, so followed his uncle to live with Liu Biao, the governor of Jing Province who governed Xiangyang(present-day Xiangyang, Hubei Province). There he lived a carefree life, but was reputed as a 'Crouching Dragon' in the social circles there. Liu Bei, who happened to be residing at Xinye County and taking shelter under Liu Biao, heard this reputation, and after three visits finally met with Kongming in 207 (12th year of Kenan).

Kongming, responding to the 'Three visits to the cottage', presented the Longzhong plan to Liu Bei, and recommended to form a strategic alliance with Sun Quan, who was based in Jiangnan, get Jingzhou and Yizhou (present-day Sichuan Province), and maintain independence, in order to compete with Cao Cao, who had conquered North China, and restore Han dynasty. Liu Bei was pleased with this plan and thought Konming as an indispensable advisor, comparing the relations with him to that of "water and fish". In 208, Liu Biao died when the army of Cao Cao moved south, and his son, Liu Cong, surrendered Jing Province to Cao Cao. Thus, Kongming wasted no time to visit Sun Quan as a emissary of Liu Bei, persuaded him to ally with Liu Bei, and in the end, brought the victory of the Battle of Red Cliff.

Liu Bei, who thus embarked on the realization of the Longzhong plan, became the governor of Jing Province, and Konming governed three commanderies such as Changsha. But, when Liu Bei moved into Yizhou in 211 and came into collision with Liu Zhang, the governor there, Kongming supported him and entered Shu, and in 214, Liu Bei occupied Chengdu and became the governor of Yizhou.

In 221, when Shu Han was established and Liu Bei took the throne, Kongming became the chancellor and supported him. But in 223, Liu Bei, who had fallen critically ill, entrusted all future matters to Kongming and died. Kongming pledged to support Liu Shan, the successor, and continued to govern the country as the chancellor. His aim was to take back the Central Plain from Wei and restore the Han dynasty with Liu family its emperor, so he reinforced the alliance between Wu and Shu, conquered different ethnic groups, which ranged as south as Yunnan, and removed the risk of being attacked from behind, and facilitated logistics. Then, starting in 227, he devoted all his energy to the Northern Expedition against Wei.

After presenting his famous "Chu Shi Biao" to Liu Shan to express his loyalty and patriotism, Kongming spent seven years in battlefields, sometimes moving into Guanzhong and threatening Wei, but in 234, when he was confronted with general Sima Yi of Wei near Wuzhang Plains (present-day southwest part of Mei County, Shaanxi province), fell seriously ill and eventually died in camp."

When I was young, I read boy's version of 'Romance of the Three Kingdoms' repeatedly and thought that Zhuge Kongming was the hero indeed.

Zhuge Kongming and Liu Bei had a strong relationship of trust.

After death of Liu Bei, Zhuge Kongming declined the throne and served for his son Liu Shan; he continued to be a "No.2". In the case of Nikai, his relationship with Prime Minister and the President of the party seems different from that a little. Nikai did not become the Secretary-General through the "Three visits" of Prime Minister Abe Shinzo. Abe asked Tanigaki Sadakazu, then the Secretary-General, to stay on the position, but because of the severe injury due to a bicycle accident, he could not do so, and as a result Nikai became Secretary-General.

Nikai was so powerful that others couldn't ignore his power, so he became the Secretary-General of LDP. The relationship between Nikai and Prime Minister Abe is different from that of Liu Bei and Kongming. Secretary-General Nikai is "No.2" of LDP, rather than "No.2" of Prime Minister Abe.

Nikai has lived his political life as the "No.2 in the conservative politics of Japan". His power of execution is so big that others cannot ignore it. In my opinion, it has been made possible because Nikai has held high moral values, noble ideals, and a sense of duty to decide the course of the country correctly.

4. Katsu Kaisyu, who devoted his energy to avoid a civil war and realized the bloodless surrender of Edo Castle

Katsu Kaisyu, who appeared on the grand stage of history during the last days of Edo Era in Japan, took the position of the Governor of Army, the highest position in Edo shogunate, by the request of Tokugawa Yoshinobu, negotiated with Saigo Takamori, the head of Emperor's Army, and realized the bloodless surrender of Edo Castle. Considering the situation of those days, surrendering the Castle bloodlessly meant protecting Edo, the biggest city in the world then, and the lives and assets of the people there from war. In addition, he succeeded in fending off the interventions from foreign countries. Indeed, Katsu Kaisyu saved Japan.

Katsu not only saved Tokugawa Yoshinobu as the "No.2" of Tokugawa shogunate, but saved the people of Edo. And a civil war between the Imperial court and the shogunate was avoided through the peaceful solution. If a total war had occurred between them, Britain and France could have participated in it. And if a war had occurred, it was highly likely that Japan would become a colony of Britain and France. Considering the diplomatic policy of the two countries then, leading Japan into a war and colonizing it was beneficial for both countries. Though, by realizing the bloodless surrender of Edo Castle, Katsu Kaisyu defended the independence of Japan.

In my late twenties, I formed "a study group of Katsu Kaisyu" and studied him. As a result, I found out Katsu was an outstanding figure.

What kind of person was Katsu Kaisyu? Here I quote the article on him from 'Asahi Encyclopedia of Japanese historical figures' (the author of the article is Matsuura Rei).

"Katsu Kaisyu was a politician in the last days of Edo Era and early Meiji Era. His true name was Yoshikuni, and nickname Rintaro. He got promotions to be Awano-kami, but after the Meiji Restoration changed his name to Yasuyoshi and made it the registered name. Kaisyu was his nickname. He was born in Edo as the eldest son of a low grade subject of the shogunate. His father, Zaemontaro (Kokichi), was best known for his autobiography, 'Musui's Story'. And one of his cousins was Odani Seiichiro who was called the Saint Swordsman. After studying swordsmanship, he moved to Dutch learning in order to pursue Western military studies, and when Perry visited Japan, he was one of the most prominent researchers on Dutch learning and military studies.

In the second year of Ansei (1855), he joined the Nagasaki Naval Academy and studied with Pels Rijcken and Kattendijke. After returning to Edo in the sixth year of Ansei, he became the head teacher of Warship Training Center, and in the first year of Man-en (1860), he sailed across Pacific as the de facto captain of Kanrin Maru. In the second year of

Bunkyu (1862), he was promoted to the deputy chief magistrate of warships. And on April next year, he accompanied Tokugawa Iemochi, the shogun then, in his inspection tour of Osaka Bay, and was permitted the establishment of Kobe Naval Training Center. He planned to make it the "shared grand Navy" of the shogunate and feudal domains of Southwest Japan and expand it as a base in East Asia to resist the invasion of Western countries.

In the first year of Genji (1864), with the establishment of Kobe Training Center, he was promoted to the chief magistrate of warships, but opposed to the conservative policy of the shogunate after the Kinmon incident on July, and on October received the order to return to Edo. Upon his arrival, he was dismissed and lost official titles. In the second years of Keio (1866), during the second Chosyu expedition, he returned to the chief magistrate of warships, and was responsible for the conciliation between Aizu and Satsuma and ceasefire negotiation with Chosyu.

In the first year of Meiji (1868), after Tokugawa Yoshinobu, who had lost in the Battle of Toba–Fushimi, returned to Edo, Katsu was promoted to the President of Army, then the Officer of military, made efforts to clean up after the former shogunate, and on the eve of total attack on Edo by the Imperial army, negotiated with Saigo Takamori and succeeded to avoid a battle.

Afterwards, he moved to Sunpu (Shizuoka) with Tokugawa family temporarily, but frequently received requests from the new government to visit Tokyo. And in the fifth year of Meiji, he was appointed Vice Minister of the Imperial Japanese Navy, then next year sangi and first Minister of the Navy. Though, he resigned due to his dissatisfaction about Taiwan Expedition of the seventh year of Meiji, and during next decade engaged in various political movements such as restoring the honor of Saigo Takamori.

In the twentieth year of Meiji, Katsu was elevated the title of hakushaku (count), then appointed as an advisor for the Privy Council next year. He kept criticizing pro-Western policies of Meiji government and advocating the alliance with Qing dynasty, and opposed to the First Sino-Japanese War. And he criticized the Ashio Copper Mine Poisoning Incident bitterly and supported Tanaka Syozo".

I think Nikai Toshihiro and Katsu Kaisyu are alike very much. As with Nikai, Katsu was a pacifist. In addition, they both are placing emphasis on Asia. Nikai has established personal relationship of trust with the leaders of Asian countries, especially those of China, South Korea, Vietnam, Indonesia, and played a great role in the friendship and goodwill with these countries.

I have confirmed the detail of this by making check in China and South Korea, and interviewing many high officials. Important persons of foreign countries love and respect him not only as a representative politician of Japan, but as a friend, and have strong relationship of trust with him. Probably there have been no politicians in the history of Japan who constructed as broad international connections as Nikai.

5. Suzuki Kantaro, a loyal subject who assisted Emperor Showa and realized the end of World War II

In 1945, Suzuki Kantaro, an aide of Emperor Showa, followed his will, restrained the Imperial Army and accepted the Potsdam Declaration, ended World War II, and saved the lives of many. Though Imperial Japan surrendered unconditionally to the Allies and lost the war, the accomplishment of Suzuki, who assisted Emperor Showa and realized peace, should be valued highly.

If he had failed to end the war on August 15th 1945, the Japanese race could have disappeared, or at least, the lives of many Japanese people might have been lost. What kind of person was Suzuki Kantaro? Here I quote the article on him from 'Asahi Encyclopedia of Persons' (the author of the article is Okabe Makio).

"Suzuki Kantaro was an admiral in the Imperial Japanese Navy, a Grand Chamberlain, and the final Prime Minister in the war period. Born in Osaka Prefecture, Suzuki graduated from the Imperial Japanese Naval Academy in 1887, and from the Naval War College in 1898. After serving in the Imperial Japanese Navy General Staff and the Navy Ministry, he was dispatched to Germany as a military attaché in 1901. Then, after duty afloat and serving as a teacher in the Naval War College, he became Vice Minister of the Navy in 1914, Commander of the training squadron in 1917, Commandant of the Imperial Japanese Naval Academy in 1918, and after serving as Commander of the IJN 2nd Fleet, then the IJN 3rd Fleet, then Kure Naval District, he became a full admiral in 1923. And he became Commander in Chief of Combined Fleet and a member of the Supreme War Council next year, then in 1925, Chief of Imperial Japanese Navy General Staff.

In 1928, he retired and accepted the position as Privy Councilor and Grand Chamberlain, serving as an aide of Emperor Showa for a long time. In the London Naval Treaty incident, which occurred in 1930, Suzuki was regarded as dove, and narrowly escaped assassination in the February 26 Incident in 1936. In the same year, he resigned Grand Chamberlain and was elevated the title of danshaku (baron). He became Vice-Chairman of Privy Council in 1940 and Chairman in 1944. On April 1945, as the course of the war got overwhelmingly disadvantageous, following resignation of Koiso Cabinet, he became Prime Minister by a strong request from Emperor Showa.

On August 14th, Suzuki accepted the Potsdam Declaration and led Japan to the unconditional surrender, after which he resigned Prime Minister. Then, he served again as the Chairman of Privy council until next year. Originally, he had not any political ambition, but was forced to become Prime Minister at the age 78. Therefore, he could be highly valued in that he resorted to extreme measures, the two Imperial Councils held on August 9th and 14th, to restrain belligerent groups within the Imperial

Army and end the war. Though, since he became Prime Minister until he declared that he would "ignore" the Potsdam Declaration on July 28th, his true intent was not always clear, so, along with the execution of the war policy by Emperor Showa, his political responsibility which brought about such disasters as the Battle of Okinawa and the dropping of two atomic bombs is still a divisive issue".

It is true that one cannot regret enough the tragedy of the Battle of Okinawa, the dropping of atomic bombs on Hiroshima and Nagasaki, and the fact that Suzuki could not end the war before the Soviet entered the war. However, the accomplishments of Suzuki, who assisted Emperor Showa and realized the end of the war, should be valued more highly.

Though Japan made a big mistake of waging a war, Japanese people now should know that there was a politician who made efforts to end it, and that Suzuki Kantaro realized the end of the war.

As a result, Suzuki saved the lives of as many as one hundred million Japanese people. It was a tragic war indeed, but Suzuki Kantaro, who ended it, was a great figure, for realizing the end of the war was an enormous challenge.

6. Miki Bukichi, a strategist-of-all-time who realized the political stability through the merger of the conservative parties

Miki Bukichi was the father of Liberal Democratic Party; LDP was formed as a result of the merger of the conservative parties. And Miki was the person who made the merger possible.

When I began to work as a freelance writer, I researched Miki Bukichi thoroughly to write his biography. I was deeply interested in his life and interviewed many acquaintances of his who were still alive at that time.

Those who knew the process of the merger thought that it wouldn't have been possible without Miki, so Miki Bukichi was a figure like "God" and "Buddha" for the politicians of LDP. However, many of young politicians now don't know even the name of "Miki Bukichi". Miki ended the power struggle between conservative politicians and accomplished the feat of stabilizing politics through the merger of the conservative parties.

What kind of person was Miki Bukichi? Here I quote the article on him from "Asahi Encyclopedia of persons" (the author of the article is Imazu Hiroshi).

"Miki Bukichi was a politician born in Kagawa Prefecture. He graduated from Tokyo Senmon Gakko (currently Waseda University) in 1904 and opened a law firm in 1912. After serving as a member of Tokyo Ushigome ward assembly, he won the Lower House election for the first time in 1917 and became the Secretary-General of Kensei Party in 1924.

During this period, when he was a member of Tokyo city assembly from 1922 to 1924, he became a powerful figure who had an influence on the politics of Tokyo city, but in 1928, he was arrested along with Syoriki Matsutaro on the charge of taking bribes from Keisei Railway, which planned to operate in Tokyo city, and was sentenced three months in jail in 1935. This case not only prevented Miki from emerging on a big stage, but after World War II, Sato Eisaku, an aide of Yoshida Shigeru, criticized this case and prevented him from becoming the Chairperson of Diet, which was his final wish. He left politics for the time being, became the president of Hochi Newspaper in 1939, and in 1942, won election as an independent candidate in the Kagawa No.3 constituency in that year's general election.

After the war, Miki participated in the formation of Japan Liberal Party, but was purged afterwards. When he returned to the political world in the general election of 1952, he supported Hatoyama Ichiro, his political rival in pre-war period, and planned to overthrow Yoshida's cabinet by forming the Separatist Liberal Party, with anti-Yoshida "Eight samurais" at its core.

On November 1954, he worked together with the Reform Party to form the Democratic Party, and on December, following the resignation of Yoshida, realized Hatoyama's cabinet, which had been his long-cherished wish. Though this change of power was driven by the criticism to bureaucratic politics, the intelligence and tactics of Miki, who threw himself into the role of Hatoyama's "military advisor", contributed greatly to it. The formation of Liberal Democratic Party on November 15th 1955 was the final endeavor of Miki, who was already seriously ill.

On March 1955, he said, "For the stability of politics and merger of the parties, we are even ready to have Hatoyama resign". And he persuaded Ono Banboku, who had been hostile to him due to the rivalry between Yoshida and Hatoyama, with his unique eloquence, and initiated the merger. When LDP was formed, Hatoyama continued to be Prime Minister, and the position of the President of the party was represented by the four deputies, Hatoyama, Ogata Taketora, Miki, and Ono. And next year, having witnessed the formation of LDP, Miki died like a withered tree. He won elections eleven times, and his highest position was a deputy of the President of the party".

About forty years ago, I contributed the biography of Miki to 'History and Figures' magazine by Chuo Koron Sha. It amounted to 100 pages of 400-character manuscript paper, but only a small part of my record on Miki could be used. I interviewed dozens of Miki's secretaries and supporters who were still alive, to discover his true image. Especially, I interviewed one of Miki's former secretaries for two days.

During World War II, Miki resisted Tojyo Hideki's cabinet, and because he was regarded by Tojyo as an enemy, retired to Shodo island in the Seto Inland Sea. In order to learn about Miki of that time, I visited Shodo island and stayed in Toyoso Hotel, where Miki had lived. After that, I spent about one year to research him, and in the end, I learned the greatness of Miki Bukichi.

Miki overthrew the cabinet of Yoshida Shigeru, who had been

filled with thirst for power and madness and lost his reason, and realized Hatoyama's cabinet. Then he realized the merger of the conservative parties, ending the struggle between them. As a result of it, Liberal Democratic Party held power as the ruling party for a long period. In addition, Kono Ichiro, a junior fellow of Miki, supported Prime Minister Hatoyama and made the Japan-Soviet negotiation a success. Furthermore, through the establishment of diplomatic relations between Japan and Soviet, Japan finally joined the United Nations and returned to the international community. This was realized after Miki's death, but in my view, it can be called a great accomplishment of Miki Bukichi, because it was him who laid a foundation for it.

I think Nikai Toshihiro and Miki Bukichi in his later years are similar very much; they both are politicians of "harmony", and at the same time politicians who always deal with things with "wholeheartedness". Miki and Nikai don't have any personal desire, always work on politics with a heart of "God and Buddha", and have a "Laozi" thought of enlightenment.

7. Nikai Toshihiro, the best and brightest statesman who has been in "No.2" position the longest

In my opinion, Nikai Toshihiro is a first-class statesman who are working on politics with the spirit of harmony and benevolence, and a deep affection for disadvantaged people.

In this section, I will analyze Nikai, who belongs to the genealogy of "No.2" figures, as objectively as in the previous sections.

Though Nikai is a super-famous figure who leads the political world of Japan, I would like to show a brief profile of him by quoting an article of 'Seikai Youran (Directory of Political World) 2019 Spring Edition'.

"When he was a member of the Wakayama Prefectural Assembly, Nikai assumed such positions as special chairperson of Kansai Airport. In

1983, he was elected to the House of Representatives, and served as Vice-Minister of Transportation in the Kaifu Cabinet. In 1993, he left LDP and joined the Japan Renewal Party. He served as Vice-Minister of Transportation again in the Hosokawa Cabinet. He was later a member of the New Frontier Party and the Liberal Party.

In 1999, he became Minister of Transportation and Director-General of Hokkaido Development Agency under the coalition administration of LDP, Liberal Party, and Komeito. Though Nikai was a close aide of Ozawa Ichiro, he transferred to the Conservative Party in 2000, the New Conservative Party in 2002, and returned to LDP in 2003. In 2007, he became Director of the General Affairs Bureau under the Abe reshuffled Cabinet and the Fukuda Cabinet. Then in 2008, he was returned to the post of Minister of Economy, Trade and Industry, and kept this post in the Aso Cabinet.

In 2012, Nikai inherited Ibuki faction to form Nikai faction. In 2014, he became Director of the General Affairs Bureau again, and was appointed the Secretary-General of the party. In 2015, he safely won the election of the House of Representatives for the twelfth time".

Though not referred to in this article, Nikai's international activities for peace are significant. Especially, the Diet members-initiated diplomatic activities of him not only supplement the diplomacy by the government, but have constructed amicable relations of trust, and have solved many difficult issues which are hard to deal with in government-level, based on his personal relations which he has established through his long-time efforts.

In this sense, I would say Nikai is the most excellent international politician in the political history of modern Japan. He has acted actively as the powerful "No.2" in the political world of Japan, and it is distinctive characteristics of him as a politician.

Both Suzuki Kantaro and Miki Bukichi were great figures, and their accomplishments are quite significant. But the period in which they acted actively was relatively short. Meanwhile, Katsu Kaisyu acted for a relatively long time, if one includes his activities in Meiji Era.

In this point, Nikai resembles Katsu Kaisyu; Nikai has acted as the "No.2" of administrations for twenty years. Considering that political achievements are accomplished through continuity, it is significant that Nikai has served as "No.2" for such a long period.

Nikai acted as the "No.2 of administration" under the cabinets of Koizumi Junichiro, Abe Shinzo (the first), Fukuda Yasuo, Aso Taro, and Abe Shinzo (the second and later). Especially under the second cabinet of Abe, after he served as Director of the General Affairs Bureau consecutively, Nikai served as Secretary-General of the party for a fourth consecutive term.

Nikai's political contributions as the "No.2" of the LDP administrations are quite big.

As well as Nikai, Zhuge Kongming, Katsu Kaisyu, Suzuki Kantaro, and Miki Bukichi didn't aspire to be "No.1" but kept serving as "No.2", lived up to their ideals, and served for the world, people, and peace. They showed leadership in the stage of real politics more than "No.1" figures and contributed to the international community. And Nikai is still active now.

8. Nikai Toshihiro, a true "No.2" who doesn't aspire to become a "No.1"

When one looks back the post-war history, there were such excellent "No.2" figures as Tanaka Kakuei and Fukuda Takeo under the cabinets of Ikeda Hayato and Sato Eisaku, and Ohira Masayoshi under the cabinet of Ikeda Hayato and Tanaka Kakuei. However, all of them aspired to be "No.1"; for them, the position of "No.2" was mere a foothold to elevate to the position of "No.1". Actually, they became "No.1". Therefore, they didn't keep serving as "No.2" without hoping to become "No.1". In this sense, Tanaka,

Fukuda, and Ohira cannot be called “real No.2”.

Also, there were such “powerful No.2 figures” as Gotoda Masaharu under the cabinets of Nakasone Yasuhiro, and Kanemaru Shin in the periods of Nakasone, Takesita, and Kaifu, but the period in which they acted as “No.2” was quite short, and their achievements as “No.2” fall short of those of Nikai.

That Katsu fended off the interference by foreign countries through the bloodless surrender of Edo Castle was a historical feat indeed. And the end of the war that Suzuki realized saved Japan. The establishment of Hatoyama Cabinet and the merger of the conservative parties realized by Miki can be called a historical feat as well. Considering that, soon after Miki’s death, Hatoyama Ichiro and Kono Ichiro made the Japan-Soviet negotiation a success, realized the re-establishment of diplomatic relations between Japan and Soviet, and accomplished Japan’s return to United Nations, the achievements of Miki are great indeed.

Nikai’s achievements are innumerable, such as the realization of tourism-oriented country, national resilience, restoration of peaceful and amicable relations between Japan and China, and development of Diet member’s and people’s diplomatic activities. And all of them are enormous feats. After Miki, there hasn’t been a “No.2” figure who achieved such great accomplishments. I will discuss about specific achievements of Nikai later, but they are surprisingly significant.

A great “No.2” figure makes history. Nikai Toshihiro is a great “No.2” who has created tourism- and culture-oriented Japan, reinforced peaceful and amicable relations with neighboring countries, realized the policy for national resilience, and constructed politics of Showa, Heisei, and Reiwa era.

Chapter 3

Nikai's political achievements which surpasses those of "No.1" figures

Nikai's significant and monumental achievements

During the thirty-seven years since he was elected to the House of Representatives in 1983, Nikai Toshihiro has always made efforts for the peace and the happiness of Japanese people. And he has realized these efforts in a way that everyone can see and they contribute to people specifically. It is no use for a politician just to speak about his policies; what he practices and how he does it based on his noble idea and belief matter. The mission of a politician is to grasp the happiness of each person from a broad viewpoint of nation and society, and to create a better world among the harsh scrutiny of people.

What a politician has achieved can be presented as how hard he has worked for the people, society, and nation. Seeing from this viewpoint of political achievements, Nikai is a strategist-of-all-time who has achieved monumental accomplishments.

One cannot list such innumerable achievements one by one. Nikai's political achievements can be characterized by their breadth. Some politicians are specialized in a particular area such as transportation, education, or health, and known as an expert of the area. It is meaningful, of course, but Nikai's activities are not limited in such a narrow scope. I will discuss about them later, but Nikai has formulated a broad scope of policies, and realized them steadily. Nikai is an excellent generalist of politics. And in each area, he has led politics as a leading expert of the area.

Then, why has Nikai been able to build up his achievements broadly and highly? Of course, his talent has been superior to that of others. In addition, he has had a strong and healthy body which can endure his energetic political activities. And Nikai is always sincere enough to tackle issues with full efforts at any time; he always pays attention, however small the matter is.

Nikai has such an excellent talent as a politician, and in addition, I keenly sense his personal distinction. He lives with moral distinction, along with intellectual distinction. Thus, he is totally unconnected with scandals, clean in a matter of money, and everyone admits his rectitude.

As for the specific aspects of his personal distinction, Nikai neither do a thing nor say a word which would hurt others. He never speaks evil of others and it is admirable.

A politician inevitably has "rivals" and "political enemies" due to the difference of opinion or standpoint. But Nikai has never had such emotional antagonism. And he will never have it.

In my opinion, Nikai has been able to accomplish many political achievements because he has a splendid personality and has lived with caring and kindness for others. Many of lawmaker-initiated legislations which he formulated were passed by unanimous votes of all Diet members. And when he was a member of opposition parties, he persuaded Diet members of the ruling party to pass some bills. To me, this fact means that he has dealt with everything sincerely, transcending the difference of parties or standpoints.

In the following eleven sections, I will categorize representative achievements of Nikai and show each of them.

1. Nikai Toshihiro, who spent 30 years to realize a tourism- and culture-oriented country

As of the spring of 2020, not only Japan but the entire world faces a crisis which arises from the spread of Covid-19. Though, it will inevitably be solved, and the tourism of Japan and the world must be revived. I believe that the tourism and culture-oriented country Japan, which Nikai has promoted, will prosper again. In any case, Nikai's great accomplishments of these 30 years will never disappear. Here we shall look back his accomplishments on tourism.

Though we are facing an unusual situation now, at a time when the goal of 40 million tourists to Japan was being achieved, it was natural to put “tourism-oriented country” policy at the center of political agenda, capturing tourism as the assets of a region or an area.

However, an idea that tourism should be put at the center of national policy is relatively new. For example, 30 years ago, most politicians thought that tourism was not their matter, and it was so indeed. In fact, few politicians had a view that tourism should be a main item of national policies.

Nikai, though, was different from other politicians; two years after he became Vice-Minister of Transportation in 1990, he was appointed as the Chairperson of Japan Association of Travel Agents. And when he became Vice-Minister of Transportation again on August 1993, he established the “Committee of 100 persons who consider the tourism of Japan”, whose aim was to exchange opinions about tourism straightforwardly and create a future image of tourism from a new viewpoint. Nikai led this committee, and Okuda Keiwa (then a member of Diet), who was a senior colleague of Nikai, and Sejima Ryuzo (then the Chairperson of the Council for tourism policies) became its top advisors. In addition, managers of tourism and transportation industry, head of local municipalities, cultural figures, and scholars were engaged in the committee, making it a full-fledged committee in which 130 persons from various fields were involved. And it was the first step for realizing “40 million inbound tourists to Japan”.

Afterwards, under the second reshuffled cabinet of Obuchi Keizo, Nikai became Minister of Transportation and Director-General of Hokkaido Development Agency. And on May 2000, he formed the delegacy for cultural and tourism exchanges between Japan and China, and visited China with 5,000 people, starting a new era of the tourism exchanges between Japan and China.

Then, on September 2002, this time as the leader of “Delegacy for friendship and cultural and tourism exchanges between Japan and China", Nikai visited China along with as many as 13,000 people, which surprised Chinese officials, and held an event to celebrate the 30th year anniversary of re-establishment of diplomatic relations between Japan and China.

In 2006, Nikai made efforts to pass the "Tourism Nation Promotion Basic Law", where increasing foreign tourists to Japan was positioned as a basic policy of the nation.

On October 2008, when Nikai was serving as Minister of Economy, Trade and Industry for the third time, Japan Tourism Agency, which was his long-cherished wish, was established. At a time when reducing and consolidating of central government agencies were a sweeping trend, under the slogan of "administrative reform", it was difficult to establish JTA. However, this agency was absolutely necessary to unify tourism policies, and its presence was vital in promoting the policy for tourism-oriented country. Thus it can be said that Nikai had the foresight in this area as well.

Then on February 2015, Nikai visited South Korea along with 1,400 people to celebrate the 50th anniversary of the normalization of diplomatic relations between Japan and South Korea. And in the same year, he visited Jakarta, Indonesia, as the leader of the "Delegation for cultural, economic, and tourism interactions between Japan and Indonesia, and held a big get-together session. Indonesia has abundant underground resources and the potential to be an important player in Asia by mid-21st century. Thus, it is meaningful to interact with such a country.

Nikai thinks that making Japan a tourism-oriented country is important for the world peace, so he has put efforts especially into the tourism industry. Nikai has always insisted that the tourism industry is the peace industry. For him, developing tourism means reinforcing "peace", so he has been advocating the "making of a tourism-oriented country". Nikai has realized it, and Japan has become one of the advanced countries of tourism. There have been few politicians who put more efforts into developing the tourism industry than Nikai, so it would not be exaggerating to say that Nikai made Japan an advanced country of tourism.

Nikai's idea to make tourism a basic national policy was appropriate one; sometimes exchanges by the people engaged in tourism are as powerful as diplomatic activities by the government.

And the power of tourism is precious now because it is a way to remedy one of the biggest issues of Japan: exhausted countryside. If tourism is promoted and more foreign tourists visit Japan, the countryside will prosper as well. In terms of its economical scale, breadth of viewpoint, and accompanying employment promotion, it can be said that tourism has become one of the essential industries of Japan. In fact, when I visit various places in Japan, leaders of every prefecture, city, and town now advocate "regional development through tourism".

Now that Japan is becoming an advanced country of tourism, Nikai makes warning advice for the people engaged in the tourism industry and the Japanese people in general. Here I quote one of his advice.

"Everyone wants tourists to come to his town and sightseeing facilities. It is natural and efforts have been made for this, but one cannot expect that tourists visit his town automatically without himself doing nothing. And local politicians also make efforts thinking that tourism means attracting tourists, but if they really hope so, they must make a journey themselves. Thus, every one of us should visit foreign countries and make a trip more actively. In my opinion, it is a theme that those who are engaged in tourism have to deal with". (From a interview with 'Kanko Keizai Shimbun' newspaper. And Morita is responsible for the wording.)

To me, Nikai's suggestion strikes home. There are various elements associated with tourism. To recognize the true value of the tourism resources which one owns, it is necessary to visit foreign countries and other areas of Japan. In short, Nikai advises that the nature of promoting tourism is to expand and continue exchanges, and he criticizes the narrow-mindedness that a lot of tourists visit only his place and bring prosperity to only his business.

A word "観光 (sightseeing)" contains a meaning of "光を観る (seeing light)". If tourism prospers in an area, this brought light to this place and brighten it. Tourism promotes peace, so it is the "peace industry" which can be developed only in peaceful countries.

By the way, I have traveled around Japan and visited almost all places. Also, I have visited many foreign countries. Though I am 87 years old now, I visited Qingdao, China, last year along with my wife. So it wouldn't be exaggerating to say that my life has been spent with journeys. And I learned a lot from that journey. One can learn only limited things from desk study, and sometimes cannot obtain the true pictures. Meanwhile, I feel that the things which I learned through journeys, from people, items, or landscapes have somehow become more ingrained.

As Nikai said, not only the people engaged in tourism, but all Japanese people should visit foreign countries and various places in Japan more and more actively. And I hope that young people who aspire to be a politician visit as many places as possible and learn a lot of things through their youthful sensibility. It is the mutual exchange with many foreigners that is indispensable for Japan to develop as a tourism-oriented country.

And especially, I would like to emphasize that one of Nikai's great achievements in his international exchange activities is the fact that he transplanted "Oga lotus" to various places in China and spread "lotus culture" across Asia.

Mr. Sakamoto Yuuji, the mentor of Nikai when he was a high school student, was a disciple of Dr. Oga Ichiro, who discovered the lotus and gave a name to it. Mr. Sakamoto committed to discovering and cultivating ancient lotuses along with Dr. Oga, and Nikai, when he served as a member of Wakayama Prefecture Assembly, got a request from Mr. Sakamoto and made efforts to create a pond of Oga lotus in the Green-Flower Center in Iwade town, Wakayama Prefecture. Furthermore, after he was elected to the House of Representatives, Nikai transplanted Oga lotus to the Hangzhou botanical garden in China to spread a campaign which aimed to support the friendship between Japan and China. In addition, it led to the construction of "Eastern Lotus Culture Garden" and "Asian Lotus Memorial Center" by the collaboration of Japan and China, and the transplantation of Oga lotus to Boao, Hainan island.

In 2004, Nikai gave a lecture at Dongbei University of Finance and Economics in Dalian, China, about "the origin of Oga lotus and the importance of grassroots exchange". Dalian is the place where Dr. Oga learned the presence of an ancient lotus from a Chinese in Pulandian District, a suburb of Dalian, when he was an instructor of the South Manchuria Railway Training Center. In other words, it is the place which led to the discovery of Oga lotus. Thus, Oga lotus awoke from 2,000 years of sleep, and lotus culture spread in Japan. A lotus researcher who resided in Pulandian heard this story, and presented Nikai a 1,300 year old seed of lotus. Then Nikai asked the Botanical Research Center of Tokyo University to bloom it, and this attempt succeeded. When I visited Dongbei University of Finance and Economics with Nikai in 2018, I was deeply impressed by the long-time relationship between him and the university, which welcomed him with a banner "Welcome back, Mr. Nikai", through this lotus culture.

Nikai's "lotus culture diplomacy" isn't limited to China alone. When a regular direct flight between Hanoi, Vietnam, and Kansai International Airport began, Nikai visited Hanoi by its first flight and learned that lotus flower was painted on old tiles which were made 300-400 years ago and unearthed in the construction site of the new parliament house.

Because lotus has survived in Asian countries as "flower of Orient", "flower of peace", or "flower of Buddhism", Nikai named this road of lotus the "road of peace" and "lotus road".

This "lotus road", through which Nikai contributed to the realization of peace by the will of his mentor, has not been known well yet, but it is nevertheless a great achievement of Nikai.

Nikai has an exquisite sense for natural beauty and has planted cherry trees worldwide; in many countries there are a beauty spot of cherry trees contributed by Nikai. And I have planted cherry trees in foreign countries with him.

In Japan as well, Nikai planted trees in the areas affected by the 2011 Great East Japan Earthquake and brightened them; Nikai has bloomed various flowers in many places in Japan.

In the early 2020, due to the spread of Covid-19, the world plunged into turmoil and the tourism industry has suffered a great loss. Both the world and Japan face a crisis, and pessimism is spreading about the future of the tourism business.

Though it is truly a big challenge for the tourism industry of the world and Japan, I think it can be overcome. When the problem of Covid-19 is solved, the tourism industry will be revived.

Now is the time for Nikai Toshihiro to play a role. Nikai is struggling at full power in order to protect the tourism industry of Japan and the lives of Japanese people. He visits various places of Japan to energize those who are struggling among hardship.

I believe that Nikai will solve this crisis, open up the way to promote the tourism industry, and show the future vision of the world and Japan.

2. Nikai's lively activities for the friendship with neighboring countries Nikai promotes peace and friendship activities with many people

For years, Nikai has worked with such neighboring countries such as China, South Korea, Indonesia and Vietnam for peace and friendship. Nikai has visited not only these Asian countries but such countries as Russia and Turkey, and continued his efforts for the world peace through the interactions with the leaders and people there.

The table below is a list of countries which Nikai has visited recently. This list, which I asked a magazine reporter, who is also a long-time watcher of Nikai, to make, includes only representative visits reported in national newspapers, and he has actively promoted peace and friendship activities many times more than that.

The list of countries Nikai has visited recently

Year	Month	Country	City
2015	2	South Korea	Seoul
	3	China	Boao
	5	Indonesia etc.	Jakarta
	5	Singapore	
	5	Philippines	Manila
	5	China	Beijing, Dalian
	10	China	Beijing
	11	Indonesia	Aceh, Jakarta
2016	3	United States	New York
	4	China	Beijing
	5	South Korea	Seoul
	7	Chile	Santiago
	7	Peru	Lima
	9	Vietnam	Hanoi
	9	Indonesia	Jakarta
	11	India	Delhi
2017	5	China	Beijing
	5	Tonga	Nuku'alofa
	5	Fiji	Suva
	5	United States	Honolulu
	6	South Korea	Seoul, Mokpo
	7	United States	Washington, D.C., New York
	12	China	Beijing, Xiamen
2018	1	Indonesia	Bogor, Jakarta
	4	Russia	Moscow, Saint Petersburg
	5	China	Dalian, Chengdu
	8	South Korea	Seoul, Panmunjom
	8	China	Beijing
2019	4	China	Beijing
2020	1	Vietnam	Da Nang

At the same time, many people visit Japan to meet Nikai. Besides these meetings, Nikai has acted for peace and friendship surprisingly actively. Furthermore, he continued these activities even when he was a member of opposition parties.

As for Diet members-initiated diplomatic activities and civil diplomacy, no one comes close to Nikai. The civil diplomacy he implements is called "human diplomacy", and at the base of it is a belief that man-to-man interactions are important, and that human relation is of necessity.

I have already mentioned Nikai's peace and friendship activities with neighboring countries, but here I would like to analyze their contents, that is, the fact that peace and friendship activities of Nikai have special characteristics unique to them. It is a wonder that Japanese media have not covered these activities sufficiently; they have covered little of them.

One of the characteristics of the delegation chaired by Nikai is that it always includes many people. Receiving countries are always surprised with its scale, which consists of as many as three thousand, five thousand, or sometimes ten thousand people.

When one wants to achieve something, there is a law that quantity converts to quality. One tends to try to get the best effect with minimum efforts, but this law indicates quality can be improved by approaching a task with overwhelming quantity. And this idea is right and correct when one implements civil diplomacy.

The delegation led by Nikai fulfills the "law of conversion" in making friendly relationship with neighboring countries. Rather than just considering how to create a friendly relationship, something great can be achieved by having many people visit neighboring country and interact with the people there directly. And it improves the "quality" of friendship. This is true civil diplomacy.

A delegation of thousands or tens of thousands of people includes various type of persons. Some are managers of companies, others are home business owners, employees, farmers, fishers, those in the tourism industry, merchants, or housewives, and they visit the country all together and meet with ordinary citizens in various places. That is, civil diplomacy is achieved naturally by a number of visitors.

In addition, the receiving country can get an enormous economic effect if thousands of people visit there. Not only this, the leaders of the country cannot help but realize that it is a full-fledged delegation with a purpose.

In fact, on May 2015, when the Japan-China relations chilled almost to freezing point by a foolish act by DPJ to nationalize Senkaku islands, Nikai led three thousand people to participate in a get-together session held in Great Hall of the People in Beijing. Then, the high officials of China confirmed through the scale of the delegation that Nikai's belief in the friendship between Japan and China was genuine one, and President Xi Jinping, in his speech welcoming the visitors from Japan, said that he would promote the friendship between the two countries.

Hayashi Motoo, who accompanied Nikai, said to me, "I think the number of the members, three thousand, made a big impact on President Xi. Probably he thought, 'Just words or visits by some politicians does not mean the friendship between Japan and China. But such a number of Japanese people come here. Japan must be willing'".

I agree with Hayashi. In order to remedy the cooled down relations between Japan and China due to the surprisingly foolish acts of DPJ, both Japan and China needed a catalyst, and it must have been impossible without a turning point. And this turning point was the delegation of three thousand led by Nikai.

Here I would like to emphasize that when Nikai visits neighboring countries with such a large delegation, its members bear all the travel expenses. They receive not a penny for participating in the delegation.

This fact is noteworthy. No one would join the delegation just from obligation. They are willing to bear the expenses because they sincerely empathize with the peace and friendship activities of Nikai. However, media has never reported this truth.

A regular attendant of Nikai's delegation told me, "Mr. Nikai is a man of emotion. If invited by him, I will attend even if it is beyond my means". Thus, Nikai's virtue attracts many people and makes a large delegate possible.

What I emphasize is that when Nikai visits neiboring Asian countries with the huge delegates, nobody pay the bill for the participants and that every participants pay for it by thenselves.

That is remarkable. Only the sense of obligation can never induce them to join the very expensive tour. Paying for the delegation responding to Nikai's call means that they sympathize with Nikai's effort for friendship and peace, which mass-media does not cover enough.

One of regular participants in the Nikai's delegates says, "Mr. Nikai is the man of sympathy. If he asks me, I will manage to join." Nikai's network attracts many people to materialize the enormous delegation.

The significance of leading such a large delegation is really big in a sense that it is true civil diplomacy. Though it is true that government leads diplomacy, true friendship cannot be developed through governmental diplomacy and that of high officials or diplomats alone. The exchanges between people must be promoted beneath it, and they have to spread among people in both countries quickly and visibly.

This Nikai has achieved by forming a large delegation including ordinary people; he has been promoting and leading people's diplomacy.

Cheng Yonghua, former Ambassador of China to Japan, told me about the friendship activities of Nikai through a large delegation.

"Though, the leaders of China and Japan agreed on the "improvement of relationship" at the end of 2014, there was an atmosphere of resignation. But the delegation of 3,000 people led by Mr. Nikai spread among Chinese people the fact that there were exchanges between not only politicians but ordinary people. Before the re-establishment of diplomatic relations, there was a slogan ‘encouraging government through the people’s power’, and Mr. Nikai spread this tradition of ‘civil diplomacy between Japan and China’ with the large delegation” (Wording by Morita).

When I interviewed Cheng at the Chinese embassy in 2018, I deeply felt that he respected Nikai as a friend of Chinese people.

There is emotion, enthusiasm, and love in the people’s diplomacy Nikai leads. And it is truly the peace and friendship diplomacy by people.

Nikai has true friends in many countries; in China, South Korea, and ASEAN countries such as Indonesia, I met a lot of politicians and high officials who respected Nikai as their elder brother.

The diplomacy of Nikai is the true “human diplomacy”.

3. Nikai led the promotion of a policy for disaster-prevention, disaster-reduction, and national resilience

Nikai has accomplished a political achievement to place a policy for “disaster-prevention, disaster-reduction, and national resilience” at the center of national politics. This accomplishment should be highly praised. Since his early days as a Diet member, Nikai was an expert on disaster-prevention policies, and when he was still a member of Wakayama Prefecture Assembly, he led such policies. Before that, he had worked for disaster-prevention when he was a secretary of Representative Endo Saburo, so it can be said that disaster-prevention is his lifework as a politician.

Recently, natural disasters have occurred frequently in Japan, and the threat of nature has attacked various places. Japan, which is one of the countries that are most prone to earthquakes, has experienced the Great Hanshin-Awaji Earthquake in 1995 and the Great East Japan Earthquake in 2011 during the post-World War II period alone. Their damage are unforgettable to many people, and some of them haven’t overcome it yet.

Nikai is a politician who pointed out the importance of disaster-prevention and disaster-reduction before anyone else and initiated specific actions. Also, when a disaster happened, he always visited the disaster-stricken area before anyone else, met with the people there, and supported them as much as possible.

When disasters happen, Nikai visits there immediately. He always does that.

After Itoigawa Large-Scale Fire which occurred on December 22nd 2016, Nikai exerted himself to designate the city as a disaster area to apply the "Act Concerning Support for Reconstructing Livelihoods of Disaster Victims". Thanks to the efforts of Nikai, if a house has been totally destroyed, the owner can receive three million yen from the national government and one million yen from the prefecture. And in a case of fire, the owner of a house has to get rid of its debris at his own expense, but if the fire has been designated as a disaster, individual payment isn't necessary. Nikai was aware of it and took measures against Itoigawa Fire based on it. And it was the first time that the act had been applied to a fire.

In an interview with me, Hayashi Motoo talked about it;

"We took measures to designate the fire as a disaster and made efforts to set the direction of aid as the national government. When it was nearly finished and I was ready to come home, Nikai told me, 'the people there must be suffering. Let's go and encourage them!'.

It was the end of the year. We flied to Toyama and arrived at Itoigawa on 31th December. Then, in the city hall, Mr. Nikai told the governor (of Niigata Prefecture) and the mayor (of Itoigawa) about the policy of the government that individual payments to get rid of debris would not be required.

He works without stopping, and visits the site before anyone else. That's Mr. Nikai."

Nikai's quick action during a disaster isn't limited to Japan only. When Sichuan earthquake occurred in China in 2008, Nikai quickly arranged a charter flight and, along with a lot of relief supplies, got on the plane and visited the affected area. Surprisingly, Nikai came back on the same day; this sense of speed is one of the characteristics of Nikai.

Furthermore, in 2018, after ten years of the Sichuan earthquake, Nikai visited the disaster-stricken area along with Diet members of the ruling parties, offered flowers on the monument of the victims, and prayed silently. I, too, accompanied him at that time, and was impressed by the fact that China preserved the traces of the earthquake to pass down lessons to future generations.

In this way, Nikai visited the affected area just after the earthquake and ten years after it. He has always lived up to a hands-on policy and acted on it; I deeply felt that he was tackling disaster-prevention, disaster-reduction, and national resilience with an extraordinary resolution. And Chinese people deeply respect him.

Among Nikai's policies for disaster-reduction, disaster-prevention, and national resilience, the significant one is the "measures against tsunami disaster". In the Great East Japan Earthquake in 2011, the tsunami that attacked the coastal areas of Tohoku district, such as Sanriku Coast, killed many people.

When the Chile earthquake occurred in 2010, Nikai had already realized that a law for the prevention of tsunami disasters was necessary. At the time when LDP was an opposition party, Nikai advocated a lawmaker-initiated legislation to deal with tsunami. Though this idea was not favored due to the opposition of DPJ, then the ruling party, "Act on Promotion of Tsunami Countermeasures" was finally passed after the Great East Japan Earthquake in 2011.

Now, "Tsunami-disaster Prevention Day" is November 5th, but some member of DPJ insisted that it should be March 11th, the day of the Great East Japan Earthquake. Though, Nikai never agreed with it, insisting on

November 5th.

I think it was appropriate. It is true that the memory of the Earthquake is still vivid to the Japanese people, and they will never forget its severeness. On the other hand, November 5th is the day when a large tsunami hit Wakayama Prefecture in 1854. Then, Hamaguchi Goryo burned the shock he had harvested to warn it early and saved many people by making them escape. In short, November 5th is the day to celebrate a successful experience, and the significance of making it "Tsunami-disaster Prevention Day" is really big. Nikai valued the successful experience of "fire on shock".

After all, Nikai's opinion was accepted, and November 5th was chosen as "Tsunami-disaster Prevention Day". And afterwards, disaster-prevention events and emergency drills has been conducted on this day, and specific nationwide movements have become established. I believe Nikai's decision was appropriate.

Then, on December 2015, Japanese government led a joint proposal of 142 countries to a committee of United Nations, and "World Tsunami Awareness Day" on November 5th was constituted unanimously. It was achieved by the efforts of Nikai and the Diet members of his faction, and the day triggered a worldwide approach to prevent Tsunami-disasters. If the "Tsunami-disaster Prevention Day" were March 11th, it would have been impossible to establish this date as "World Tsunami Awareness Day". It was because November 5th was the day of a successful experience that it could get worldwide approve. Again, one can see Nikai's foresight.

However, Nikai didn't stop at developing such laws and establishing "World Tsunami Awareness Day" in United Nations. Nikai is always looking at the future; he thinks that in Tsunami-disaster prevention, nothing is more important than education, and has initiated the educational activities for it worldwide.

After the establishment of "World Tsunami Awareness Day", high school students from thirty countries gathered in Takashio town of Kochi

Precture in 2016, and held "'World Tsunami Awareness Day' high school students summit". And similar summits were held in Okinawa next year and in Wakayama Prefecture, the stage of "fire on shock" in 2018, in which students from 48 countries and districts participated. During this summit held in Wakayama, the students of Hidaka High School, the alma mater of Nikai, acted as the chairperson of the committee and held discussions voluntarily.

In these days when various disasters such as concentrated downpours, earthquakes, and abnormally fierce heat have occurred frequently, "national resilience" is an imminent political issue. Disasters of recent years have occurred in unexpected areas or scales. To save the lives and assets of people is now a common belief across Japan; "disaster-prevention, disaster-reduction, and national resilience" have become the central policy of Japanese government.

However, such belief was not common in the past.

In present Japan, it has become justifiable to take various kinds of measurements based on the idea that even if a disaster occurs, not a life should not be lost. And it is achieved by Nikai. Even when no one thought national resilience as the biggest basic policy of the nation, he strongly insisted that we make a nation where not a life would not be lost even in a disaster. Such politicians as Nikai whose basic ideal is "not a life should be lost" can be called a genius statesman.

Nikai has lived up to this ideal, felt his mission as a politician and as a human, and devoted himself on realizing it. Such efforts were rewarded with the establishment of "Basic Act for National Resilience Contributing to Preventing and Mitigating Disasters", and a system have been developed in which national efforts are made for taking measurements against various disasters, doing evacuation activities during a disaster, and maintaining important social infrastructures which guards and develops the economy and lives of people. In addition, the awareness of people to disaster-prevention and disaster-reduction is increasing.

And Nikai has said, "the nature of disaster-prevention, disaster-reduction, and national resilience is that they are not a responsibility of the central government and local public authorities alone. Rather than just protecting his own life from natural disasters such as earthquake and tsunami, each of the people should think what he can do to protect precious lives of others, and how to care for and support the disaster-stricken people".

This kind of view is important indeed. If people just entrust everything on politicians or the government, true disaster-prevention, disaster-reduction, and national resilience can never be achieved. Through the policies by the government, each household and each person should be convinced that they have to lead a life in which they are facing natural disasters.

I believe Nikai is right, so I strongly hope that he plays a more active role at the front line of politics as the leader of people.

4. Nikai's significant contribution to the restoration of LDP-Komeito coalition administration—The period between August 30th 2009 and December 16th 2012

On August 30th 2009, the coalition of LDP and Komeito lost the Lower House election, DPJ won it, and the change of administration was achieved. Then, 17 days later, the DPJ cabinet of Hatoyama Yukio was formed.

December 16th 2012 is the day when the DPJ cabinet of Noda Yoshihiko was trounced in the Lower House election and DPJ administration ended. The coalition group of LDP and Komeito won the election and returned to power. And 10 days later, December 26, the second cabinet of Abe Shinzo was formed. Afterwards, Abe administration won three Lower House elections and three Upper House elections, and has become a long-lasting cabinet.

In the election held on August 30th 2009, Aso Taro administration was totally defeated. LDP won only 119 seats, Komeito 21 seats, while DPJ won as many as 308 seats, and LDP left from the position of a ruling party. It was such a total defeat that the opinion dominated that LDP would never return to power; it was widely thought that even if possible, it would take more than decade for LDP to return to power. Almost no one thought that LDP would regain power just in three years and three months.

Hatoyama Yukio, the new Prime Minister, became the big star of the political world of Japan, and Ozawa Ichiro, mighty Secretary-General of DPJ, acted as if he were a dictator. In the fall of 2009, the "Hatoyama-Ozawa" regime seemed invincible and long-lasting; no one expected that, just after nine months, Prime Minister Hatoyama and Secretary-General Ozawa lost their position like double suicide. In those days, it was commonly believed that DPJ administrations would last forever.

I have an unforgettable memory.

On one evening of January 2010, I visited the headquarters of LDP to meet Nikai, then the chairperson of LDP General Survey Committee for National Resilience, and Hayashi Motoo, its vice chairman. However, though it was a weekday, the building was dark, for the lights had been turned off. And at the reception desk was a security guard alone. I walked along the dim corridor and got on the elevator. When I got off it at the fourth floor, but no one, even reporters, was in evidence. And except the room of the General Survey Committee for National Resilience, which situated just in front of the elevator, the lights of all other rooms were turned off. In addition, the committee used the office of Election Campaign Committee chief temporarily.

Inside the room were Nikai and Hayashi alone; there were no staffs in the room.

The headquarter building of LDP was like a haunted house. I visited Nikai and Hayashi several times after it, and the situation was always the same.

Afterwards, I asked a veteran stuff of LDP why the lights were turned off, saying, “if the building is dark, the morale will remain low. At least, why don’t you turn on the lights?” The stuff answered, “if we turn on the lights, the bank officers will say, ‘if you have enough money to turn on the lights, pay back the debt’. We borrowed too much money in an ardent desire to win the election. Because the bankers believe that we will never win again, so they keep after us to pay back the debt. Though, only Mr. Nikai doesn’t get upset when bank officers come. So only the room where Mr. Nikai is present is bright”.

In those days, even bankers believed that LDP would never return to power.

Indeed, a change of power gives a severe blow to the losers. Before losing power, the headquarter building of LDP was full of people all day long. The visits of lobby groups from all over Japan never ceased, and the officials of central ministries and newspaper reporters scrambled to visit the headquarters of LDP.

However, when LDP lost power, these people disappeared instantly. The lobby groups crowded the headquarters of DPJ, and the officials of central ministries changed their destination; if it was found out that they had visited the headquarters of LDP, now an opposition party, they would be derailed from a career track. And reporters turned their back on LDP. Though I saw several reporters who respected Nikai as a compassionate politician, it was a sad sight indeed.

Such atmosphere spread among the party as well, and many members of both Lower House and Upper House rarely visited the headquarters. In addition, almost all of Diet members of LDP just thought about defending only their own position, and few sought to bring LDP back to power.

However, there were several politicians who made efforts to realize LDP’s return to power.

One was Ibuki Bunmei, a former Secretary-General and the leader of Shisuikai faction (the predecessor of Nikai), who became the speaker of the Lower House after the election in 2012. Ibuki explored a shape of LDP's future and worked on the "mission statement of the party" for a new generation. And through it, he exerted himself to strengthen the leadership of the party over its Diet members.

And another was Nikai, who explored national resilience. I cooperated with him on his "study of national resilience" by attending conferences, making speech, and writing articles.

There was a deeper reason for my cooperating in national resilience. I studied and researched Marxist economics in my university days, but after becoming an editor specializing in economics, I studied Keynesian economics and insisted that Japan should follow a path of modified capitalism. Then, when I became the editor-in-chief of 'Economics Seminar' magazine, I got acquainted with Uzawa Hirofumi, who had just come back to Japan from United States, and asked him to write articles on the magazine regularly. At some time or other, I became intimate with him so much that we frequently went to pubs and drank beer. Though Uzawa was an economist of Keynesian economics, he made efforts to surpass it, and what he was considering was the reformation of economics itself. As such, Uzawa was a bright scholar with a big vision.

It was in early 1973 that I was given a title of "political commentator" and entered its world, and since then, I have advocated Keynesian economics in discussing economic policies. It was because I thought that modified capitalism was best suited for Japan, but since 1980's, Japan has been affected strongly by the revolution of neoliberalism which was emerging in U.S. and U.K., and such trend as "supremacy of free competition", "from the bureaucracy to the private sector", and "reduction of public projects" got momentum. Thinking that abnormal denial of "public projects" was dangerous, I criticized the wrong tendency of Japanese politics which valued neoliberalism highly and kept pointing out the danger of too much shift to neoliberalism by writing 'An Essay on the Necessity of Public Projects' and 'A New Essay on the Necessity of Public

Projects'.

And it was Nikai Toshihiro who supported my first essay both publicly and privately. He used his deep and large connections to held parties to celebrate its publication nationwide. As a result, the book became a bestseller and the publisher thanked me much. When the denial of public projects was dominant in the political world, it was so courageous an act of Nikai, who was one of the highest officials of a ruling party, to support my opinion.

However, due to lack of my power, these books could not change the trend of the political world to deny public projects; my efforts fell. I still regret that I could not reciprocate the kindness of Nikai.

In 2011, after 10 years after my publication of 'An Essay on the Necessity of Public Projects', Fujii Satoshi published 'An Essay on Resilience of the archipelago' and received support from ordinary people. And the one who paid attention to Fujii's theory was Oshima Tadanori, then the Secretary-General of LDP, which had become an opposition party. Oshima asked Nikai, who is a peer of Oshima, to become the chairperson of "General Survey Committee for National Resilience". Nikai accepted the offer after thinking a whole day; it was a wise decision.

At first, the member of the committee was just Nikai, the chairperson, and Hayashi Motoo, the vice chairperson, but later Fukui Teru joined and became its secretary-general. Though Fukui belonged to Kochikai faction (then Koga faction of LDP, and now Kishida faction), he decided to act as an ally of Nikai, left Kochikai, and after having acted as an unaffiliated Diet member, joined Nikai faction. Now he is one of the important allies of Nikai.

During an early period of General Survey Committee for National Resilience, it was mere a meeting of Nikai Toshihiro, Hayashi Motoo, and Fukui Teru. But after Nikai decided to draw up "Basic Act on Tsunami Disaster Management", over 10 Diet members of LDP and Komeito joined the committee voluntarily. And Nikai, an official of an opposition party, succeeded in persuading DPJ, the ruling party, and passing the law unanimously through his extraordinary capability of politics, large and deep connections, convincing power, and his own “art”.

When Nikai began to work on national resilience, Komeito was just making a policy called “New Deal for Disaster-Prevention and Disaster-Reduction”. The officials of both parties, which had cooperated in creating and passing the Basic Act on Tsunami Disaster Management, unified “New Deal for Disaster-Prevention and Disaster-Reduction” by Komeito and the “national resilience” policy by LDP, created the draft of “Basic Act on Disaster-Prevention, Disaster-Reduction, and National Resilience (abbreviated name)”, and submitted it to the Diet as a lawmaker-initiated legislation. Though LDP and Komeito had already persuaded DPJ when they were opposition parties, the bill was passed after they returned to power.

LDP and Komeito passed not only “Tsunami” and “Disaster-Prevention, Disaster-Reduction, and National Resilience” bills, but also the bills for “Countermeasures Against Nankai Trough Earthquake” and “Countermeasures Against Tokyo Inland Earthquake”, and both parties became intimate in the process. Strong relations of trusts emerged between the officials of both parties, and Nikai was in the center of them.

Nikai spread discussions on national resilience among the entire LDP, and it improved the leadership of LDP headquarters and restore a sense of unity in the party.

After losing the election held on August 30th 2009, LDP broke up. The sense of love for the party faded and the leadership of the headquarters weakened. It was Nikai’s “General Survey Committee for Disaster-Prevention, Disaster-Reduction, and National Resilience” that changed this tide. At first, the committee was a meeting of Nikai, Hayashi, and Fukui alone, but all the Diet members of LDP joined it soon.

While LDP organized the system of the party and strengthened the power of togetherness through the efforts of such persons as Nikai and Ibuki, DPJ suffered from breakups and disintegrations. After both Hatoyama Yukio and Ozawa Ichiro, the first leaders of DPJ administration, fell from power as a result of power struggle, Kan Naoto, the next Prime Minister, and Ozawa came into collision, and Ozawa, along with the members of his faction, left DPJ led by Kan, and the party broke up. Kan decided arbitrarily to raise consumption tax, and as a result DPJ was defeated in the Upper House election in 2010. It was a suicidal act. While DPJ won only 110 seats combined with the seats uncontested, opposition parties and other political groups won 131 seats. DPJ lost a majority.

Noda Yoshihiko, the third Prime Minister of DPJ administration, solicited by such anti-China politicians as Ishihara Shintaro, did foolish acts of discarding pacifism, which must be defended at any cost, creating a conflict around Senkaku islands, and destroying the peaceful and friendly relations between Japan and China. Furthermore, he arbitrarily decided to raise consumption tax without any agreement within the party and lost the support of people. And in 2012, Prime Minister Noda dissolved the Lower House at the worst timing for DPJ; the party broke up as if detonating itself. As a result, the coalition of LDP and Komeito returned to power.

Though it can be said that the biggest cause for the coalition administration was the folly of DPJ leaders, the convulsive efforts of the veteran Diet members of both parties were also important. Especially, sincere efforts of such persons as Nikai, who passed a lot of important bills as members of opposition parties, should be valued highly.

After the landslide victory in the Lower House election held on August 30th 2009, the leaders of DPJ fell into raptures. They lost their reason, repeated unrestricted factional struggles, and fell together. In the end, DPJ lost all like the grasshopper in an Aesop's fable. On the other hand, the politicians of LDP and Komeito, which had lost power, worked hard single-mindedly like ants. Day after day, they met and dialogued with people, thought out what to do for the people, and made their efforts. And at the front of these efforts was Nikai Toshihiro. In my opinion, Nikai contributed the most to LDP and Komeito's return to power.

By the way, I have some advice for politicians, especially for the leaders of opposition parties; learn from Nikai how to live as a politician. The leaders of opposition parties have too strong "ego". However, Nikai is always unselfish, discarding his ego and living up to peace, benevolence, and generosity. I recommend the leaders of opposition parties to have Nikai as their mentor and start again from the beginning.

The politicians of LDP and Komeito, especially the leaders of both parties, endured those three years and three months, since the defeat on August 30th 2009 until the victory on December 16th 2012, with their unyielding spirits. And Nikai realized the return to power with his indomitable optimism.

Now, Nikai is concerned about the "arrogance" and "slackness" of a long-time rule of the government, and is aware that LDP administrations have entered into a period of trial. To me, Nikai seems to recognize that a critical moment is approaching.

5. Nikai's ardent efforts to eliminate unjust discrimination

Nikai Toshihiro is a politician of goodness and justice. Even in his youth, he resolved that he would eliminate unjust discrimination which still remained in the world.

The most representative discrimination in Japan is the Buraku problem. It is by no means a matter of the past. There are those who are suffering from unjust discrimination even now.

Nikai have known more profoundly than anyone else that it is a mission of politicians in a law-governed country to eliminate discrimination with the power of law. And he has struggled to realize a legislation to solve the Buraku problem.

I interviewed Yamaguchi Tsuyoshi, who had played a central role in the lawmaker-initiated legislation of "Act on the Promotion of the Elimination of Buraku Discrimination", and learned the process of it in detail. The paragraphs below are based on the documents and testimonies of Yamaguchi, but I am responsible for the wording.

As for the laws on Buraku problem, there had been no legal basis since a special measures law had expired in 2002. A "pro-human right bill", which LDP administration had submitted in 2002, was scrapped, and DPJ submitted a "bill on establishing a human right committee" in 2012, but it was also scrapped by the dissolution of the Lower House. Through this, one might assume that a lot of politicians understood the necessity of a legislation for eliminating discrimination, but these facts shows how it was difficult to pass such a bill as an actual act.

In the meantime, "the special committee on discrimination problems" was established in LDP, and "the subcommittee on Buraku problem" under it. Yamaguchi became the chairperson of the subcommittee. It was Nikai who appointed Yamaguchi, his confidant, as the promoter of this difficult task. From the fact that he appointed Yamaguchi, who has bright intelligence and extraordinary energy, as the chairperson, one can see Nikai is a good judge of character.

Nikai, then General Affairs Council chief of LDP, told Yamaguchi, "Make it a bill and go forward. It must not be scrapped". Nikai encouraged Yamaguchi to pass the bill, which had been scrapped as a result of the dissolution of the Lower House, and Yamaguchi met his expectation.

Preparations to turn the bill into legislation was not easy one. They interviewed the representatives of related organizations and prominent figures over and over, and considered the details of the legislation. There were many problems such as how to establish a "human right committee" and whether punitive clauses and financial clauses should be included. And finally, the bill was submitted as "Act on the Promotion of the Elimination of Buraku Discrimination" to a regular Diet session on May 2016, which reads that "the Buraku discrimination must be never tolerated and must be resolved. Let's resolve the Burake discrimination." However, there wasn't enough time to pass it in the Upper House by the completion of the Diet session, so they didn't have it passed in the Lower House and tabled it for further discussion. Thus, the discussion was resumed in the extraordinary Diet session of the autumn, and the bill came to a vote at a meeting of the House of Representatives Judicial Affairs Committee on November 16th, and was approved by an unanimous vote except the Communist Party. It can be said that Nikai's word "It must not be scrapped" realized the legislation. Yamaguchi told me that he remembered vividly seeing tears in Nikai's eyes.

And the bill was passed in the plenary sessions of both the Lower House and Upper House, and promulgated on December 16th. Nikai's long-time wish took a form of legislation and make a big step forward towards eliminating discrimination.

At a glance, Buraku problem is a domestic issue of Japan. But President Trump repeats discriminatory remarks shamelessly, and hate speech cases became more frequent. In a situation where the world order has become more fluid and ethics has been lost markedly, the enactment of "Act on the Promotion of the Elimination of Buraku Discrimination" in Japan can be a message to the world to create a society without unjust discrimination, so its significance is really big.

The fact that Nikai Toshihiro, a politician of justice who has the idea of egalitarianism, has worked hard to eliminate discrimination and made a big step forward by selecting Yamaguchi has a great significance not only for Japan but also for the world.

The one who realized this ardent hope of Nikai was Yamaguchi Tsuyoshi, an ally and disciple of him.

While acting as a Diet member for a long time, a lot of lawmaker-initiated legislations by Nikai have been enacted. This "Act on the Promotion of the Elimination of Buraku Discrimination" is also one of the legislations Nikai has drawn up, but it is the act for which Nikai exerted himself the most.

Here I quote the whole text of the act.

(Translator's note - the English text was quoted from the website of IMADR, a NGO-group which promotes actions against discrimination and racism)

Act on the Promotion of the Elimination of Buraku Discrimination
Adopted by the Diet on 9 December 2016

(Purposes)
Article 1 In the light of the fact that Buraku discrimination still exists even today and that the situation of Buraku discrimination has been changed along with the increased use of information technologies, and given the importance of the challenge to eliminate Buraku discrimination on the basis of the recognition that such discrimination is not acceptable in line with the principles of the Constitution of Japan, which guarantees the enjoyment of fundamental human rights for all citizens, the present Act aims at promoting the elimination of Buraku discrimination, by establishing the basic principle and defining the responsibilities of the State and local governments in relation to the elimination of Buraku discrimination as well as by providing for the consolidation of advisory mechanisms and other measures, thereby realizing a society free from Buraku discrimination.

(Basic principle)
Article 2 The measures concerning the elimination of Buraku discrimination shall be taken with a view to realizing a society free from Buraku discrimination, by seeking to improve the understanding of each and every citizen on the need to eliminate Buraku discrimination, in accordance with the principle that all citizens shall be respected as unique individuals who enjoy fundamental human rights on an equal basis.

(Responsibilities of the State and local governments)

Article 3 (1) In accordance with the basic principle set out in the preceding Article, the State shall be responsible for taking measures concerning the elimination of Buraku discrimination as well as for providing necessary information, guidance and advice for the promotion of such
measures by local governments.
(2) In accordance with the basic principle set out in the preceding Article, local governments shall seek to take measures, consistent with their local conditions, concerning the elimination of Buraku discrimination on the basis of appropriate division of roles with the State and in collaboration with the State and other local governments.

(Consolidation of advisory mechanisms)
Article 4 (1) The State shall take measures to consolidate mechanisms to respond to requests for advice and support concerning Buraku discrimination in appropriate ways.
(2) Local governments shall seek to take measures, consistent with their local conditions, to consolidate mechanisms to respond to requests for advice and support concerning Buraku discrimination in appropriate ways, on the basis of appropriate division of roles with the State.

(Education and awareness-raising)
Article 5 (1) The State shall conduct necessary education and awareness-raising in order to eliminate Buraku discrimination.
(2) Local governments shall seek to conduct necessary education and awareness-raising, consistent with their local conditions, in order to eliminate Buraku discrimination, on the basis of appropriate division of roles with the State.

(Surveys on the actual situation of Buraku discrimination)
Article 6 With a view to contributing to the implementation of the measures concerning the elimination of Buraku discrimination, the State

shall conduct surveys on the actual situation of Buraku discrimination in collaboration with local governments.

< Supplementary provision >
The present Act shall come into force as from the day of promulgation.

Among the significances of this act, the first is that Article 1 (Purpose) clearly states, "given the importance of the challenge to eliminate Buraku discrimination on the basis of the recognition that such discrimination is not acceptable in line with the principles of the Constitution of Japan, which guarantees the enjoyment of fundamental human rights for all citizens".

The second is that Article 2 states "realizing a society free from Buraku discrimination".

The third is that the act requires the State and local governments to take measures concerning the elimination of Buraku discrimination (Article 3).

The fourth is that it clearly states that the State and local government shall "conduct necessary education and awareness-raising in order to eliminate Buraku discrimination".

Nikai has solved one of his long-time issues in this act.

Many of you readers should know the existence of this act, but might not have had a chance to read it thoroughly. Here I hope you to do so. Especially, those who are engaging in politics and those who aspire to be a politician have to explore it.

6. Nikai has supported Eastern medicine for a long time—

He has exerted himself as the top advisor of the association of acupuncturists and massage practitioners

Nikai has detailed knowledge on medicine and medical care, both Eastern and Western, and made efforts publicly and privately to protect the health of people through the collaboration of Eastern and Western medicine.

There is one thing the West and the East have in common; an idea that "health" is "the most important for human". Aristotle, a philosopher who played a great role in forming Western civilization, defined in his 'Nicomachean Ethics' the happiness of human as follows:

"The first is 'health', the second 'to be with his beloved', and the third is "to live with a heart of God'".

In short, "health" is the prime element for a happy life.

The purpose of social activities of human is to realize "goodness" in this world. Aristotle defined the purpose of politics as the realization of "Supreme goodness". Here "Supreme gooness" means "the happiness of people", so politicians have to make efforts to realize it. In other words, protecting the happiness of humankind is the most important issue of politics.

"Health" is the most important thing in Eastern civilization as well. In 'Zhou Li', the most important literature of the ideas of ancient China, it is said that the purpose of politics is to realize "health, happiness, harmony, affinity" and "happyness, longevity, health, restfulness".

The meaning of the former is that the purpose of politics is to create a society where people can live a long life healthily and peacefully. The latter has similar meaning that the happiest thing in this world is to live a healthy long life both physically and mentally.

"Zhou Li" means the "Rites of Zhou". It is said that the creator of Chinese Confucianism is Confucius, but there was a saint politician whom he respected. It is Dan, Duke of Zhou who was active 500 years before Confucius, and Dan aimed to make a peaceful country where people can live a long life healthily and happily. Confucius inherited and evolved this ideal of Dan, and 'Analects' is the literature which consists of the dialogues between him and his disciples.

As such, health is the most important thing in China as well.

The view that health is the important for the survival of humankind does not differ in the West and in the East. Therefore, medicine and health care, which save a life and maintain health, have been thought as the most important things in human societies. However, they have evolved in a different way in the West and in the East.

In the West, medicine was formed based on the religious idea of Judaism, Christianity, and Islam, and the scientific idea since the age of ancient Greece. The most significant characteristics of Western medicine is that a human body is understood as an aggregate of various parts of body such as brain, heart, gastrointestine, and limbs. And it is based on the idea of protecting a life by curing or removing affected parts.

On the other hand, Eastern medicine is based on the idea of maintaining health by keeping the balance of one's whole body. Thus acupuncture and moxibustion have evolved in the East which maintain health by energizing the flow of "chi".

Meanwhile, massage has been evolved in both the West and in the East as an effective way of maintaining health. Due to this historical context, massage is classed as Western medicine in the medical system of Japan today, while acupuncture and moxibustion as Eastern medicine.

Chinese medicine was introduced in ancient Japan through Korean Peninsula. Then it was transformed to Japanese-style medicine, evolved to medicine unique to Japan, and take root in Japanese society.

Though, when medicine from Holland was introduced to Japan during mid-Edo era, a strong tendency was developed in the shogunate to promote Western medicine. As a result, Kampo medicine from China and Western medicine from Holland coexisted during the last days of Edo era.

After Meiji Reformation, the government adopted a policy to put Western medicine in the center of medical care. The general trend of civilization and enlightenment can be seen in medical aspects as well. Medical faculties of imperial universities and medical schools were established to expand medical education, but all its contents were about Western medicine. For a time the Meiji government adopted an extreme policy that excluded Eastern medicine, so Eastern medicine, which had supported the health of Japanese people for 2,000 years, died down. However, the power of tradition was strong, and Kanpo medicine survived among ordinary people; thanks to the efforts by a few promoters of Eastern medicine, it could persist.

However, history repeated itself. Soon after the surrender of Japan on August 15th 1945, Japan was occupied by the Allies including U.S. The Occupation authorities tried to ban Eastern medinine and unify the medical care in Japan into Western medicine. Though, courageous practitioners and researchers of Eastern medicine opposed it fiercely and it could survive. Japanese people, too, used traditional Eastern medicine in their daily life to maintain their health.

Despite it, the trial for Eastern medicine continued. In the healthcare insurance system established after World War II, it suffered from unjust discrimination. While Western medicine, supported by the healthcare insurance system, was popularized widely, Eastern medicine was excluded from the system. It makes a big difference whether the healthcare insurance would be applied to a medical treatment. Eastern medicine, to which the healthcare insurance was not applied, was in a very disadvantageous position. In spite of this fact, acupuncture, moxibustion, and massage have been persisted thanks to a strong demand of ordinary people and dedicated efforts by the practitioners and researchers.

And it was Nikai who stood up to support acupuncture, moxibustion, and massage. Nikai has wide knowledge on the history of Eastern and Western medicine; he is surprisingly knowledgeable.

In order to eliminate discrimination against Eastern medicine, Nikai has supported it as the top advisor of the association of acupuncturists and massage practitioners.

Nikai, who understands the suffering of acupuncturists and massage practitioners better than anyone else does, has exerted himself to improve the legal system in health, welfare and labor administration to create a system where people can use Eastern medicine easily.

It was more than twenty years ago that Nikai became the top advisor of the association. Generally speaking, when a politician agrees to become an advisor of an organization, it would be an important factor whether they would support him in elections, no matter whether he is aware of it or not. Though, Nikai doesn't have such interests and has supported the association and the practitioners of Eastern medicine including acupuncture, moxibustion, and massage.

In short, Nikai has supported the association privately in order to improve the health of people and support "the world and people".

Though not conspicuous, this achievement of Nikai is really big, because caring for such suffering people is beneficial for all people in that it improves their health.

In my opinion, this is a significant achievement of Nikai as a politician. Usu Syosei, the President of Wakayama Prefecture Association of Acupuncturist and Massage Practitioners, and Secretary-General of all Japan League for Acupuncturist and Massage Practitioners, told me of his deep gratitude and respect for Nikai. I think Nikai is great in that he has been making efforts for Eastern medicine without considering his own interest.

Nikai is respected by many acupuncturists and massage practitioners as God or Buddha.

7. Nikai Toshihiro, an unparalleled genius of "election" in the political world of Japan

Election is the basis of democratic politics. When one wants to be a member of an assembly, he has to win the election. A politician who is not adept at elections cannot be a great figure in politics however excellent in other fields.

There is a saying often mentioned in the political world in the past: "A monkey is a monkey even if it falls from a tree, but a politician becomes an ordinary person if he lose the election".

Election has a great significance not only for politicians but also for parties, because the fate of a party depends on the result of election.

When looking back on the political history, the existence of professionals and advisors of election has had a great importance. When I became a political commentator in 1973, the top officials then were all strong in election, and at the same time excellent professional of it. Among them, Prime Minister Tanaka Kakuei was thought as No.1. In those days, LDP had such figures as Hashimoto Tomisaburo, Secretary-General, Takeshita Noboru, Chief Deputy Secretary-General, Ishida Hirohide, Chief of National Campaign Headquarters, Ezaki Masumi, Acting Secretary-General, and Okuno Seisuke, General Affairs Council chief. They were all professionals of elections and strong at their own election as well. Meanwhile, many of the officials who were thought strong in election belonged to Tanaka faction, and Tanaka was especially strong among them. Tanaka fought elections with emotion; in those days, multiple-seat constituency system was adapted in Japan, but it seemed to me that Tanaka had thorough knowledge on the electoral situation. And Tanaka himself had constructed a grass-root base in his own constituency.

Nikai, a disciple of Tanaka, is the most excellent inheritor of Tanaka's art in election. What Tanaka and Nikai have in common is an idea that the most important thing in fighting an election is the love for the people. Nikai, too, has thorough knowledge on the electoral situation all over the country under the single-member district system of today.

There is a saying which past professionals of election used often: "If you know the enemy and know yourself, you need not fear the result of a hundred battles. If you know yourself but not the enemy, for every victory gained you will also suffer a defeat. If you know neither the enemy nor yourself, you will succumb in every battle". It is the essence of the Art of War by Sun Tzu.

Until 1990's, professionals of election had learned the classical theory of tactics by such figures as Sun Tzu, Machiavelli, and Clausewitz. They studied modern social psychology and an area called "psephology". Of course, both Tanaka and Nikai have had thorough knowledge on them.

However, election is not just a science. To use the words of Bismarck, it is an "art". If one cannot use "art" along with "science", he cannot be called a professional of election. However, Nikai understands both "art" and "science".

Now is the age of opinion poll, and its accuracy has been very high. Especially, opinion polls for an election uses large samples and are analyzed thoroughly.

Some Diet members perform their own opinion surveys in their constituency regularly. And not a few politicians perform opinion surveys on their rival candidates and consider the strategies and tactics for the election.

As an election campaign approaches the final stage, some candidates make a plea to the leader of their faction or the top officials of their party, saying, "My votes will be five hundred fewer than those of the rival candidate". However, no top officials today can provide them these five hundred votes, except Nikai. He can do it through his wide and deep connections which he has constructed around Japan.

The LDP officials who lead election campaigns are Secretary-General and Election Campaign Committee chief. Though Nikai is Secretary-General and the general director of elections, he has been frequently engaged in election campaigns as a election campaign advisor even if he didn't have such a title.

However, there were some campaigns where Nikai was not engaged, and the result was a complete defeat for LDP. The example is the Upper

House election in 2007 and Lower House election in 2009. LDP fought the Upper House election in 2007 under Abe Shinzo administration, but the defeat led to the collapse of the first Abe cabinet. And the Lower House election in 2009 was held when Aso Taro was in power, and the defeat brought an end to LDP administration. It was the first time since the formation of LDP that it suffered such a catastrophic loss.

Without efficient leaders and advisors, a party can never win an election; under a mediocre leader, victory in election cannot be attained.

In the Lower House election held in 2009, DPJ won 308 seats; it was a landslide victory and the party achieved the change of power, its long-cherished wish. Meanwhile, LDP won only 119 seats and lost power.

From 2007 to 2009, I was asked several times to support DPJ candidate. When the Upper House election was held in 2007, I received a lot of such requests and visited various places to support those candidates. And in the Lower House election in 2009, when I was requested to support some DPJ candidates, I supported only those whom I regarded as trustworthy.

By the way, I have lived up to "friend first" policy since my youth. It can be called "humanity first" policy. During those years in which I have been engaged in political activities, I have sticked to this friend first policy and regarded the humanity as the basis of trust. I have put more emphasis on one's humanity than which party he belongs or what kind of policy he advocates. Therefore, I have declined to support DJP candidates when a trustworthy friend of mine in LDP runs for the same constituency as his rival. Conversely, even if such a friend is LDP candidate, I support him if requested. This is my way of life.

I acted as a leader of left-wing students' movement in my youth. Since then, I have lived up to the friend first policy and befriended those who can be relied on as a human. No matter what anyone says, I have maintained such a way of life until now. I have lived thinking that I would be willing to die for friendship. It might sound arrogant of me to call a genius statesman like Nikai “a friend of mine”, but for me, he is really an invaluable friend of mine.

Nikai is a genius of election and has established a strong support base in his constituency. I believed that even if LDP suffered a crushing defeat and most of LDP candidates lost in the election, Nikai would absolutely win; I have never been concerned about his election campaign and its result.

However, on August 28 2009, just two days before the election day, a media person who is also a friend of mine told me that a survey said Nikai was going to lose. Though I thought it unlikely, I departed for Wakayama without thinking.

I owed a great debt to him in publishing my ‘An Essay on the Necessity of Public Projects’, and had never forgot it. So, I couldn’t help but do something.

On the evening August 29th 2009, when I arrived at Tanabe station, there was a campaign car of candidate Nikai in front of it, and he had taken to the streets. Most of the audience seemed to sincerely hope Nikai’s victory.

As I was walking among the audience, I met with several officials of central ministries whom I was acquainted with. When I asked them why they were there, they answered that they had gotten a leave of absence to support Nikai. Hearing it, I keenly felt Nikai’s personal magnetism again. I approached the campaign car to greet him and asked him that I give a campaign speech. He agreed it, so I got up to the roof of the car and spoke to the audience, “Mr. Nikai is an important politician for Japan. There are no politicians in Japan who are more important than him. Please support and vote for him”.

Afterwards, I took a car ride together with him and accompanied him until the end of the campaign of the day. On eight o’clock p.m., Nikai made a heartfelt speech.

“I truly appreciate your attention. Whatever results follow, I have only gratitude for you. I thank you from my heart”.

His expression was clear as if he had understood everything. Seeing this scene, I realized again that Nikai was a figure as great as Saigo Takamori.

As I had expected, Nikai won a landslide victory, rather, he didn't lose and kept his seat.

I found out later that the faction of a leader of DPJ had spent big sums on a negative campaign against Nikai and developed it thoroughly. They even deployed a lot of groups to support DPJ candidates, but they all ended up in failure and added up to nothing.

Nikai overcame all kinds of sabotage and won the election. I left Wakayama early morning next day and returned to Tokyo. Then, I learned Nikai's victory.

Since returning to power in 2012, the second Abe administration has kept winning national elections. And in my view, Nikai is the man who has contributed the most to these successive victories.

Here I show you the results of the elections after 2012

(the Lower House election in 2012)

LDP: 294 seats (119 seats in the previous election), Komeito: 31 seats (21 seats) / DPJ: 57 seats (308 seats)

(the Lower House election in 2014)

LDP: 291 seats, Komeito: 35 seats / DPJ: 73 seats

(the Lower House election in 2017)

LDP: 284 seats, Komeito: 29 seats / Party of Hope: 50 seats, The Constitutional Democratic Party of Japan(CDP): 55 seats

(the Upper House election in 2013)

LDP: 65 seats (50 seats in the previous election), Komeito: 11 seats (9 seats) / DPJ: 17 seats (47 seats)

(the Upper House election in 2016)

LDP: 56 seats, Komeito 14 seats / The Democratic Party (DP): 32 seats

(the Upper House election in 2019)

LDP: 57 seats, Komeito 14 seats / CDP: 17 seats, Democratic Party For the People: 6 seats

After World War II, it is the first time that a ruling party or a ruling coalition has won three consecutive victories in the Lower House elections and three consecutive victories in the Upper House elections as well, in total six consecutive victories in national elections.

The driving power behind these successive victories is the electoral cooperation of LDP and Komeito. And Nikai has acted as the pivot of this cooperation.

Nikai has played a role of Zhuge Kongming in the coalition administration of LDP and Komeito. As long as he remains in its center, there will be no chance for opposition party to show off.

There is one issue for Nikai, and it is the training of his successor. In the conservative parties of Japan, Miki Bukichi was followed by Tanaka Kakuei and Tanaka by Nikai Toshihiro.

The peak of Miki's activities was in 1955 and that of Tanaka was in 1972. And Nikai has been active as the most powerful leader, though in the "No.2" position, for twenty years from 2001 until today.

In the political world of Japan, a genius politician has emerged every twenty years. I expect that next savior of the conservative politics will appear around 2030 - 2040, but I hope it realizes earlier than this. I wish the appearance of new genius politician who inherits Nikai's wisdom, spirit , and "art" as a politician.

8. Nikai has promoted enhancement of the party prestige and restoration of party's fiscal health as Secretary-General

Diet members are busy; every day they are engaging in the Diet activities in Tokyo and his political activities in his constituency. He might be engaged in Diet members-initiated diplomacy. Among them, the hardest task for them is enhancement of the party prestige, which means increasing the number of party members. Today, as people's distrust for political parties gets harsher and harsher, expanding the party prestige is more difficult than ever. It is common to all parties, but only LDP and Komeito has achieved it steadily. The reason is the firm attitude of the party leaders. Especially, that of LDP leaders is very uncompromising. The enhancement of the party prestige has faced some difficulties these days, but as long as Nikai, a person of wisdom, acts as Secretary-General, it is not impossible to overcome them.

As of 2017, the number of party members of LDP was 1,068,560, and increased by 24,770 compared to the previous year. Furthermore, the number had increased for five consecutive years. About 70% of the LDP Diet politicians fulfilled the quota to get 1,000 party members. They are the results of the fact that Party leaders had strongly encouraged all its Diet members. Nikai, the central figure of the party leadership, said, "I have used every opportunity to tell the Diet members that they themselves have to pay attention to increasing party members, and its momentum is becoming genuine. I will tackle it continuously".

In the hope of restoring the party prestige, LDP started the "campaign to attain 1.2 million party members" in 2014, and instructed to all its Diet members to retain more than 1,000 new and existing party members. And although there had already existed a penalty that if one could not achieve it, he would be fined 2,000 yen per one member, new penalty was added in 2017 that his name would be revealed. Nikai is by no means indulgent.

Here I compare the number of members of major parties as of 2019.

LDP: app. 1,100,000
Komeito: app. 400,000
CDP: Unknown
Democratic Party For the People: app. 76,000

Japanese Communist Party: app. 300,000 people
Nippon Ishin: app. 19,000
Social Democratic Party: app. 15,000

Even given the fact that the party has just been established, CDP's "unknown" is too irresponsible as a political party. Furthermore, CDP is the leading opposition party. Thus its leaders have to be aware of its responsibility as a political party.

LDP had as many as 2-5 million members in 1990's, and it was more than 5 million in 1991. However, when a non-LDP administration led by Prime Minister Hosokawa was established in 1993, the number decreased sharply.

When LDP lost the Lower House election on August 2009 and left the position of a ruling party, the number of its members dropped to the lowest level. Though, after it won the Lower House election on December 2012, the party prestige restored gradually, and after Nikai became General Affairs Council chief, then Secretary-General, the number increased clearly and exceeded one million in 2016.

Among Secretary-Generals of the past, Nikai is most enthusiastic about enhancing the party prestige. So as long as Nikai-regime continues, it will be likely that the number of LDP members exceeds 1.2 million.

By the way, annual membership fee of LDP is 4,000 yen(2,000 yen for family members), and that of Komeito is 3,000 yen (2,000 yen for support members, plus 1,887 yen monthly as subscription fee of the party paper 'Komei Shimbun').

In the multiple-seat constituency system of the past, the power of the supporters' groups of LDP Diet members was enormous. In early 1970's, when I started reporting LDP, it was said that there were 8-10 million supporter's of LDP Diet members, compared to 1 million party members.

And in late 1970's, a system was established where ordinary party members could participate in the election of the party President. And at one election, the first vote was done by only ordinary members, and the final vote in which the top two candidates participated was done by only its Diet members. This system increased the number of party members sharply; those who had just been a member of a supporters' group joined the party as an ordinary member. A period when the number of party members was 2-5 million was realized by numerous members of individual supporters' groups joining LDP.

In the LDP President elections today, both Diet members and ordinary party members have 50% of votes. If, as in late 1970's, only ordinary party members can vote in the first round of the election (and only Diet members can vote in the second round), the number of party members may be increase greatly, for many people assume that winning in the LDP presidential election means becoming Prime Minister.

In order for democratic politics to function, the relationship between people and politics has to be closer. Toward this goal, the leaders of each party should make more efforts to increase its party members. And in this, LDP and Komeito is doing relatively well.

It may be exaggerating, but I'd say that the only ones who tackle this issue sincerely are Secretary-General Nikai, Acting Secretary-General Hayashi Motoo, and a few allies of them.

In order to increase the number of party members, one has to make politics more trustworthy and improve the level of the political world as a whole. And especially important is the relationship between political ethic and people. Therefore, I believe political spirit of Nikai is required now.

Under Secretary-General Nikai, the finances of LDP has improved significantly. In 2009, when Aso Taro was in power, LDP borrowed heavily from banks to prepare for the Lower House election, but suffered a crushing defeat and lost power. As a result, bureaucrats, local governments, and media people all abandoned LDP. The business community, which had been a close ally of LDP for a long time, also kept distance from the party.

As I wrote before, more and more people who saw the landslide defeat of LDP came to think that the party could never return to power again. Banks gave up on LDP, too, and harshly urged it to pay back the debt; the officials of banks, seeing the light of LDP headquarter building turned on, said, “If you have enough money to turn on the lights, pay back the debt for us”. Bankers hit a dog fallen in the water without mercy.

The finances of LDP scraped bottom, depriving its Diet members, staffs, and party members of their morale.

It was a group of veteran Diet members such as Nikai Toshihiro, Ibuki Bunmei, and Hayashi Motoo, who displayed an unyielding spirit in such a situation. Their spirit had never been defeated.

It is subsidies to political parties, contributions, and business income such as fund-raising parties that support the finances of LDP. The party doesn’t rely on the subsidies only, and gets contributions and business income, but the trend of subsidies shows the change of the party finances.

The table below shows subsidies to LDP, Komeito, and DPJ from 2006 to 2018.

Subsidies to political parties

Year	LDP	Komeito	DPJ	CDP
2006	168	28	104	-
2007	165	28	110	-
2008	158	27	118	-
2009	139	26	136	-
2010	102	23	171	-
2011	101	22	168	-
2012	101	22	165	-
2013	145	25	85	-
2014	157	26	66	-
2015	170	29	76	-
2016	174	30	93	-
2017	176	31	78	4
2018	174	29	55	27

(hundred million yen)

It shows the big significance the change of the power in 2009 gave on the finances of each party.

LDP revived financially as well. Political donation returned to past levels and the party finances became normal. And it was largely due to the efforts of Secretary-General Nikai and his allies.

Under Secretary-General Nikai, the finances of LDP are healthy and steady; Nikai is good at financial operation as well, like a first-class executive. He knows how to save and spend money.

It cannot be denied that the party prestige has started to crack since 2019. Politics tends to fall into disarray at the end days of a long-time administration and even LDP administration is no exception. A time of trial for Nikai is approaching. However, I believe he will overcome it.

9. Nikai keeps pursuing the politics of "peace, benevolence, and tolerance"

When I accompanied Nikai in his international and domestic activities and saw him do "goodness" for others, I always remember a phrase: "It is the duty of government to make it difficult for people to do wrong, easy to do right".

It is a word by Gladstone, a liberal politician of England in the nineteenth century.

Seeing Nikai's political activities in which he treats every person fairly, I strongly feel that he is essentially a seeker of "goodness"; Nikai is a truly good man.

As long as human societies exist, the battles between good and evil never cease. This is a never-ending battle, and Nikai is a guardian deity of "goodness".

Nikai is a politician of "peace". His energetic activities for making Japan a "tourism and culture-oriented country", which he has been engaging in for thirty years, are aimed at realizing the peace of Asia and the world. And he has made efforts to develop friendly relationship between Japan and such nations as China, South Korea, Vietnam, and Russia in order to guard the world peace.

In addition, Nikai's efforts for disaster-prevention, disaster-reduction, and national resilience are aimed at protecting the lives of Japanese people and make Japan a peaceful and safe country. Among the politicians in Japan today, Nikai is the one who has exerted himself the most for realizing the peace; I don't know any other politician who has made as many efforts as Nikai.

Nikai has a resolution that he will keep living up to his beliefs as a politician of peace.

There is an idea of peace, benevolence, and tolerance at the basis of Nikai's politics, and "tolerance" here means the endless caring for ordinary people.

As for such a belief of Nikai, not all of the world takes it favorably. Unfortunately, there are warmongers in this world indeed. In addition, various disaster may hit the humanity in the future. It can be said that Nikai's politics of "peace, benevolence, and tolerance" will be facing a great trial in 2020.

The global situation is unstable and natural disasters occur frequently. A new type of pneumonia caused by Covid-19 plunged the world in turmoil. And a grim reality is in front of us such as ethnic conflict, racial conflict, expanding of various social divides, and a vicious cycle in which evil creates evil. The political and economic situation in United States, China, Europe, and Middle East is unstable, and even Japan is not safe.

Now, both the world and Japan need Nikai Toshihiro, a politician of "peace, benevolence, and tolerance". Age doesn't matter to a politician. In 'Book of the Later Han', there is a saying "be going strong despite one's age".

I sincerely hope Nikai will be active as a lifelong politician and keep working for the peace of Japan, Asia, and the world.

10. Nikai's measures against Covid-19 which are based on a long-term viewpoint

When it was reported that Covid-19 infection was spreading rapidly in Hubei Province, Nikai reacted to it quickly, collected masks and protective suits and sent it to China. Furthermore, he requested Koike Yuriko, the governor of Tokyo, to send to Chine some of the masks which Tokyo Prefecture had stored, and this request was realized.

Chinese people was greatly thankful for this quick support activity and it has a significant meaning to the development of friendly relationship between Japan and China.

Afterwards, the infection of Covid-19 began to spread around Japan as well, and China supported Japan with masks, protective suits, and so on. This is due to the friendly relationship created by the early support from Japan. The promoter of this movement was Nikai; he acted behind the scene while saving face of the government. He persisted in his way.

Nikai is always looking into the future.

Among the turmoil caused by the global spread of Covid-19, Nikai and his allies has analyzed domestic and international situations calmly and studied the strategy and tactics for the future so that the government of Japan should not commit mistakes.

In 'Analects', there is a saying by Confucius, "If you don't consider the distant future, you will sorrow before long".

Nikai's political activities are always based on a long-term view. He has made political decisions and made efforts to solve real problems by looking into the distant future, and is still doing so.

As of March 2020, the situation is quite uncertain. As for such problems as what is "Covid-19", or how we can stop its epidemic and save the lives of the affected, clear solution has not been discovered yet. Medical people and stuffs of all administrative bodies are groping in the dark.

Nikai has a wisdom which he has developed through his political experience; he never fails to make a decision which the Secretary-General of LDP should make. And when the government needs advice, he gives it properly.

Again, Nikai always prepares for the future and studies hard what kind of long-term view Japan should have among the coming upturn of world politics and world economy.

2020's will be an age of upheaval, and Covid-19 can alter the history totally.

We Japanese have to endure in this age of upheaval, and ruling parties are responsible for protecting the lives and asset of people. Nikai is keenly aware of this political responsibility and studying the measurements for the future. At the same time, he is supporting those researchers who are developing the vaccine to contain Covid-19; Nikai has some excellent researchers in his connections.

The measurement against Covid-19 is not a matter of one country but a challenge which the whole world faces now. Neighboring countries and nations around the world have to cooperate and support each other to overcome this difficult situation. And in such a time, daily friendship between countries displays its merit. In this sense, Nikai is the top statesman who has constructed friendly relations with foreign countries.

Japan now requires politicians who has a long-term view and live up to pacifism. Especially, when the world faces great challenges and struggles, Nikai's wisdom is truly needed to overcome them.

11. The cooperation of Japan and China to cope with "Covid-19 problem"—Nikai's support for China and Alibaba's support for Japan

The world is suffering from the infection of Covid-19 and Japan is no exception. Japan faces a severe shortage of masks. Both the governments and companies are working hard on increased production and importing of masks, but these efforts haven't met the demand.

In such a situation, Miyauchi Hideki, a member of the Lower House, told me a heartwarming episode about Nikai's long-time friendship with China.

Miyauchi acts as a Deputy Secretary-General of LDP now, and a member of the cabinet committee in the Lower House, has exerted himself to pass "Act on the revision of the Act on Special Measures for Pandemic Influenza and New Infectious Diseases Preparedness and Response".

Miyauch is a white hope of young Diet members of LDP and is known for his acting power. He took his time to visit me and told me how Jack Ma, the founder of Alibaba Group, one of the biggest IT company of China, had contributed one million masks to Japan.

When thousands of new cases of Covid-19 were detected every day in China and there was a severe shortage of medical supplies, Jack Ma took counsel with Nikai, his long-time acquaintance, about securing these supplies. In response, Nikai quickly arranged 125,000 medical protective suits and send them to China.

To reciprocate this, Ma contributed one million masks to Japan and sent a letter to Nikai. Here I quote the whole text of it. (The translation was provided by Miyauchi, and I'm responsible for the wording)(Translator's note: The English version is translated from Japanese text of the book)

> To Mr. Nikai, whom I respect.
>
> After a month of the battle with Covid-19, we Chinese people could finally overcome the worst time.
>
> When the infection spread and the severe shortage of medical supplies in China became imminent, I asked Mr. Nikai to find medical supplies for China. And I vividly remember your reply, "If relatives are ill, it is natural to support them. We will gather together the power of our nation and support China".

Afterwards, you kindly approached in all quarters and provided 125,000 protective suits for the medical stuffs in China who were fighting in the front line to deal with Covid-19 cases.

We Chinese were all moved by numerous and heartfelt supports from Japan.

Unfortunately, Japan, too, faces a grim situation now. This time, we Chinese, who know the difficulty, strongly hope to support Japanese people at any cost.

So we secured one million masks emergently and decided to entrust them to you. Please distribute them to medical institutions in need of medical supplies. I sincerely hope that Japan win the battle against Covid-19 as soon as possible.

These masks were collected by Alibaba Foundation and Jack Ma Foundation together. However, they contain not only the feeling of Alibaba but that of many Chinese people. We truly thank you for the support Japanese people gave us and would like to reciprocate it.

Now, we are fighting against the same difficulty, and I believe we will support each other and overcome difficulties together.

I wish the peace of Japan and China and express our gratitude again.

I wish the health of Japanese people from my heart.

Alibaba Foundation
Jack Ma Foundation
Jack Ma

In a cardboard box containing the masks, there was a Chinese poem which meant “we are neighbors who see the same mountain, so let’s overcome difficulties together”.

In response, Nikai sent a letter to Jack Ma.(The text was provided by Miyauchi)

Dear Mr. Ma,

The news that you are kindly contributing us one million masks has encouraged Japan and Japanese people. I express my gratitude for you quick decision and kindness.

Against the epidemic of Covid-19, both Japan and China are working hard to prevent its spread and end it.

In Japan, we face a shortage of sanitary supplies such as mask, and not only medical institutions but daily lives of the people are affected by it. So the government and Liberal Democratic Party are exerting themselves to overcome this difficulty.

In such a situation, the masks you kindly contributed have already arrived in Japan and have been distributed to various places where masks are needed. Gratitude is arriving from all quarters and I appreciate the deep relationship between Japan and China.

The tourism and economic interactions between Japan and China, which we have constructed overtime, are temporarily in hardship, but I believe that we will defeat this infection and the bond between Japan and China be stronger further.

I express my gratitude again and wish you good health and success.

Secretary-General of Liberal Democratic Party of Japan
Nikai Toshihiro

Nikai, the honorary chairman of Internationalization of Medical Services Association (IMSA), sent the contributed masks to medical institutions and relating organizations in need of them.

The kindness and caring of Japan and China, long-time neighbors, is contained in these one million masks, and their warm friendship will be a great power to overcome this difficulty which the world faces now.

Now, nothing is more important than worldwide cooperation.

Everyone should seek mutual objectives while ignoring minor differences. Antagonism must be discarded at any cost.

The friendship between Nikai and Jack Ma, the founder of Alibaba Group, is precious one.

First of all, the people of Japan and China should cooperate and construct a worldwide collaborative framework.

Epilogue

Investigating unique political philosophy and methods of Nikai Toshihiro

Nikai has lived up to a saying "Who knows most, speaks least"

In the viewpoint of achievements as a politician, Nikai is unrivaled. As I pointed out in this essay, he accomplished uncountable number of achievements such as realizing "tourism-oriented country", implementing "disaster-prevention, disaster-reduction, and national resilience" policies, driving "diplomatic activities initiated by Diet members", making efforts to "eliminate social discrimination", "re-evaluation of Eastern medicine", "successive electoral victories", "enhancement of the party prestige and restoration of finances of the party", and strengthening the "coalition administration of LDP and Komeito". No one has achieved such numerous political accomplishments other than Nikai.

65 years ago, when the conservative parties merged, Miki Bukichi, who was called a genius of politics, ended the confusion during the last days of Yoshida administration and realized the merger. Based on this, he set a political direction to realize a negotiation between Japan and Soviet Union and joining of Japan to United Nations, but when they were realized successfully, Miki had always passed away. Though the merger of the conservative parties can be called a historic feat, he didn't achieve other political accomplishments; he passed away as soon as this feat. Though it was a Heaven's will, I regret that Miki's genius could not be used for the people any longer.

And 50 years ago, Tanaka Kakuei, another genius of politics, conquered a fixed notion to attach too much importance to school background, which was widespread in the world of politicians and bureaucrats, becomes a Prime Minister of common people, and moved politics closer to the people. This achievement should be valued highly. In addition, he accomplished the re-establishment of diplomatic relations between Japan and China, which had not been progressed during the Sato administration, establishing a flow toward peace in Asia. Then, facing the oil crisis, he initiated Japan's own diplomatic policies and made efforts to save Japanese economy.

These political achievements of Tanaka are extraordinary indeed, but unfortunately, the politics of Tanaka ended there. The attacks by the political circle of U.S. hindered the way to make use of Tanaka's natural ability for the people. It was unfortunate for both Japanese people and Tanaka himself that his great talent was made to be used for the restoration of his own honor only. As well as the political circle of U.S. then, politicians and media people of Japan who cooperated it made a big mistake.

If the plan for remodeling the Japanese archipelago which Tanaka proposed had been carried out, it would have stabilized Japanese economy after its high growth, but it was unfortunate for Japan that it was hindered by the oil crisis and following stagflation, though they were accidental. Soon after this, when a shift in economic policies was required, Tanaka entrusted the steering of them to Fukuda Takeo, his political rival. This deed of Tanaka can be valued highly; a politician should ignore his personal emotion and Tanaka practiced it.

Compared to the political methods of Miki and Tanaka, that of Nikai is moderate and unspectacular. However, it seems to me that this fact proves Nikai is a person who "knows most, speaks least"; he has checked himself at all times, and without bragging about his political achievements, sticked to serving for the people.

Looking back on the 65 year-history of LDP, one finds there have been several "No.2" politicians who has enormous power. From 1960's to early 70's, Tanaka Kakuei and Fukuda Takeo acted as "No.2", but they were just in this position on the way to becoming a top leader.

From 1980's to early 90's, Kanemaru Shin and Gotoda Masaharu exerted a great power as "No.2" politician, but they left almost no political achievements which could be called historical. They had political power but not significant ideal and policies.

Nikai's political achievements are extraordinary, because he holds his ideal and pursue a policy based on it. This fact should be evaluated fairly; the achievements of a politician have to be evaluated based on its contribution to the people and society.

After World War II, Japan have followed the way of parliamentary democracy, and three genius of parliamentary politics have appeared during these 65 years: Miki Bukichi, Tanaka Kakuei, and Nikai Toshihiro, all party politicians.

Among these three politicians, Nikai's political method is unique. He has acted as inconspicuously as possible so that the public eye would not concentrate on him. He has lived up to a idea of "three treasures (tendresse, humility, and not aspiring to be the top) of Laozi.

Buffon, a French naturalist of 18th century, said "genius is perseverance", and Nikai has extraordinary perseverance.

An excellent politician uses his "art"

"Politics is not science but art", a saying by Bismarck, is often used in political circles. "Politics is an art of possibility" is also quoted often as a saying by Bismarck, but it is not clear whether these sayings are really by him. However, "art" is a word which he used frequently.

Not only politicians are engaged in politics; bureaucrats, political reporters, and scholars are engaged in it as well. However, only leading political figures can use "art" adequately. Bureaucrats, political reporters, and scholars haven't been trained to use it. Though some of them understands the politicians who use "art", but their number is a few. Ordinary bureaucrats, political reporters, and scholars cannot understand the "art" of leading political figures.

Nikai understand this "art" well and use it adequately to make important decisions; he is a master of "art".

Miki Bukichi, too, shook hands with his political rival Ono Banboku in order to realize the merger of the conservative parties. He was a master of "art" in that he did what nobody could expect.

Tanaka visited China to realize the re-establishment of diplomatic relations between Japan and China, and met with Zhou Enlai and Mao Zedong. It was a bolt from the blue, so it can be said that Tanaka used his "art" as well.

In 2010, when Nikai was a member of an opposition party, he established a league of Diet members for measurements against Tsunami, promoted a lawmakers-initiated legislation for promoting measurements against Tsunami, persuaded the ruling DPJ which opposed to it, and finally passed the bill unanimously both in the Upper House and the Lower House; he accomplished the impossible. Furthermore, as a result of his efforts, November 5th, the day of "fire of shock", was designated as "World Tsunami Awareness Day" in UN General Assembly. And as for "disaster-prevention, disaster-reduction, and national resilience", he initiated the preparation for its legislation when he was a member of an opposition party, and following LDP's return to power, passed it in 2013. By using his "art", Nikai achieved what people regarded as impossible.

One cannot move politics just by the power of science, which forms a hypothesis and pursues the truth. It can be said that the "art" of a politician is necessary to look straight at a reality and achieve something. Leading political figures have their own "gut feeling". Nikai have been able to initiate such dramatic politics because he knows how and when to use his "art" better than anyone else.

Nikai Toshihiro, an inheritor of "Wakayama Spirit"

As I mentioned before, travel have been the center of my life for 87 years. I visited almost all major cities in Japan, and though I have traveled abroad just about 20 times, I went to all areas of Japan except some distant islands.

I have traveled to Wakayama several hundred times and visited most places of historical interest and scenic beauty several times. And about thirty years ago, I studied some of historical figures from Wakayama

Prefecture, especially Tokugawa Yoshimune, Hanaoka Seisyu, and Minaka Kumagusu.

Though born in Wakayama, Tokugawa Yoshinobu became the 8th shogun of Tokugawa shogunate. He was born in 1684 and pass away in 1751.

Hanaoka Seisyu, a surgeon of late Edo era, studied both Eastern and Western medicine, managed to invent a kind of anesthetic, performed an operation on breast cancer, and made a great contribution to the medicine in Japan. He was born in 1760 and passed away in 1835.

As I wrote before, Minakata was a naturalist and folklorist of Meiji, Taisho, and Showa era, and was called a genius. He discovered 70 new species in his study on Myxomycete and was a world-class genius whom Japan was proud of. Minakata was born in 1867 and passed away in 1941.

Nikai was born two years before Minakata passed away; he inherited Minakata's genius. And in my view, Nikai is the inheritor of "Wakayama Spirit" these historical figures of Wakayama held.

I met Nikai for the first time in late 1980's. It was at a party of Okuda Keiwa, a member of the Lower House and an officer of Tanaka faction, whom I had been acquainted with since 1973. At the party, I sensed that there was a genuine politician and Nikai would be a leading statesman representing Japan; I saw a "genius of politics" in Nikai.

Nikai was born on February 1939, and I feel somewhat strange seeing the list of period these four figures lived.

Tokugawa Yoshimune: 1864-1751
Hayaoka Seisyu: 1760-1835
Minakata Kumagusu: 1867-1941
Nikai Toshihiro: 1939-

Hanaoka, the genius of medicine, was born nine years after Tokugawa Yoshimune, the genius of politics, passed away. Minakata, the genius naturalist, was born thirty-two years after Hanaoka passed away. And Nikai, the political genius of present, was born two years before Kumagusu passed away. Since Edo era, Wakayama Prefecture produced a world-class genius once in a hundred years.

Again, when I met Nikai for the first time, I sensed that he is a political genius, and have paid attention to his life as a politician for more than thirty years.

Though associating Tokugawa Yoshimune, Hanaoka Seisyu, Minakata Kumagusu, and Nikai Toshihiro as great figures born in Wakayama is my subjective view, I feel that Wakayama Spirit has been inherited through them and see Nikai as the "genuine inheritor of Wakayama Spirit.

In the past, I studied Tanaka Kakuei and contributed articles on him to a general magazine in 1970's and 80's. Upon requested to contribute articles, I visited Tanaka's constituency in Echigo district of Niigata Prefecture and interviewed its citizens and farmers. And one time, I collected opinions of several hundred people to write an article comparing Tanaka and historical figures of Niigata.

In the end, I found out Tanaka was respected more than any other great figures. In fact, Tanaka loved and cared for the people of Niigata more than great figures of the past (Uesugi Kenshin, Ryokan, Maejima Hisoka, and Yamamoto Isoroku, for example) did. And the people of Echigo understood Tanaka Kakuei.

Nikai has essentially the same personality with Tanaka, but the political method is more moderate. Nikai is a politician of "harmony" and have made efforts for the world peace more than any other present politicians have. In addition, he always seeks "harmony" in everything.

Nikai's political method focuses on "the middle course and balance". A person as powerful as Nikai would be able to treat Wakayama specially, but Nikai never forces something and operates politics considering the whole balance at any time.

"Wakayama Spirit" is easygoing, and it might be because Kii Peninsula is mainly facing south. I feel that Nikai's energetic activities as an international politician is related to its open climate.

What underlies Nikai's spirit as a politician

What underlies Nikai's spirit is a caring for everyone.

All the people have more or less such a caring. However, on rare occasions, those who have a limitless caring and exert it appear.

And one of these persons is Nikai Toshihiro. In order to exert a limitless caring, one must have great courage, acting power, and ability to achieve something. Nikai has been able to exert a limitless caring because he has strong belief and acting power.

However, the world situation is rapidly changing now, and politics which holds such a caring is facing a big barrier. Can Nikai overcome it? Frankly speaking, the barrier which Japan faces now is very thick. But Nikai has to overcome it and I believe he can do it.

Now, both the world and Japan face an enormous difficulty and the human society is shaken by the severe change in the natural environment. Grudge and distrust are swirling in the world of human. In the battle of "good" and "evil", "good" begins to be driven away. In addition, vicious cycle in which evil produces evil emerges in some places, and there is even a possibility of war.

As well as all of these, a phenomenon of disintegrating ethic emerges and is spreading. The human society faces a trial, and now, the world is suffering from Covid-19.

Also, Japan's politics is facing enormous difficulties.

How will Nikai Toshihiro, a politician who has limitless wisdom and lives with the people, overcome this crisis?

If requested from Nikai to cooperate in a new challenge for establishing peace, I will work hard despite my old age.

Afterword

On the fall of 2019, I reached the age of eighty-seven. And looking back my life, I feel that one's life is the history of his human relationship.

In my memory, I met Nikai Toshihiro for the first time at a party of Okuda Keiwa, a member of the Lower House and a senior colleague of Nikai, and it was about thirty years ago. Okuda is a top member of Tanaka faction who served as Minister of Transport, Minister of Home Affairs, Minister of Posts and Telecommunications, and so on. In addition, he was a straightforward politician who recalled a saying "Sturdiness and quietness is his virtue", worked with such politicians as Hata Tsutomu, Ozawa Ichiro, and Watanabe Kozo, and ended his political life as a DPJ member of the Lower House. He, five years older than me, was born in the war period and one of the benefactors of my life.

One time, Okuda told me an episode about Nikai: on the fall of 1983, Tanaka Kakuei told Okuda to support Nikai, who was prepared to run in the next election from Wakayama.

Then, Okuda said to me, "Kaku-san(Tanaka) took notice of Nikai. It was remarkable that Kaku-san paid special attention on a freshman lawmaker".

Soon afterwards, when I asked Kojima Hiroshi, my friend and a secretary of Gotoda Masaharu, then the chief Cabinet secretary, whether he knew about Nikai, he answered, "Yes, I know him. He participated in the first University on the Ocean which we were on board".

The first University on the Ocean is a workshop on the sea held on the spring of 1973, in which LDP gathered its hopeful young politicians. Then, I was on board the ship as an instructor by the request of Secretary-

General Hasimoto Tomizaburo. Hearing from Kojima that Nikai had been on board as well, I sensed that he and I have a kind of affinity. And it was more than ten years after this that I met Nikai directly.

It was Professor Yoshimura Tadashi, a political scholar, who introduced me to Secretary-General Hasimoto Tomisaburo, and Professor Shimizu Ikutaro who introduced me to Professor Yoshimura. Professor Shizimu was my mentor in the period of the protest campaign against Sunagawa U.S. military base.

I met Okuda Keiwa for the first time at the office of Secretary-General Hashimoto in 1973.

And when I saw Nikai for the first time, I felt that I finally found an ideal politician whom I had sought for a long time; seeing his good nature, kindness, humility, and politeness, I thought he was the one who had appeared in this world to be a politician in the best sense, and I met an ideal conservative politician at last. In that moment, I became an admirer of Nikai, not just a fan.

It was when the Great Hanshin earthquake occurred that I sensed the extraordinary talent of Nikai as a politician; though he was a member of an opposition party, he visited the affected area faster than any other Diet members did. Although the Murayama cabinet then did relatively well some time after the disaster, but its first motion was slow. At that moment, Nikai took a courageous act and encouraged the entire political world. Afterwards, I have followed his political activities.

There are some LDP Diet members who deserve respect, and here I introduce three of them.

The first is Ibuki Bunmei. I get acquainted with him in 1989, about thirty years ago from now. He is a person of integrity, have excellent intelligence, and excels in ethics and intellect. He has so excellent character that I would recommend him as the next Prime Minister. Ibuki has served as the former chief of Nikai faction and the speaker of the

Lower House, and now leads the LDP as the top advisor of Nikai faction.

The second is Hayashi Motoo, and I respect him from my heart. He is a person of who can be called a “man of sincerity”.

Studying personality, especially that of leaders, is one of my studying themes. I have heard from a lot of their allies a saying, “the leading figures who is important for a organization the most should not be placed in a solitary situation”. Nikai is a precious leader not only for LDP but also for Japan, and Hayashi has been always with him and never left him alone. Few can do such a thing so he reminds of me a saying “All the great figures are humble”(Lessing).

The third is Yamaguchi Tsuyoshi. He has good character and high ability, and is an excellent politician who will be a leader of the political world in the near future.

Many excellent politicians with “goodness” such as Ibuki, Hayashi, and Yamaguchi supports Nikai. I sincerely hope that they continue to work for the people of Japan and the peace of the world.

In my opinion, there have been three persons who can be called “Mr. LDP” in its history: Miki Bukichi, Tanaka Kakuei, and Nikai Toshihiro. And Nikai’s achievements rival or surpass those of Miki and Tanaka. Nikai is a politician of the people who represents present Japan.

Last but not least, I would like to say this: Nikai is the great genius statesman who has represented the political world of Japan of 20th and 21st century. The father of his spirit is Tanaka Kakuei, and the mother is Minakata Kumagusu.

What I sensed the moment I met Nikai for the first time was, “This man was born to this world to do good politics for the world and people”. This feeling hasn’t changed a bit for more than thirty years since the first encounter.

The reason I regard Nikai as a genius politician is that Nikai has a talent to read human mind precisely. This is the feeling which I sensed about Miki Bukichi when studying him to write his biography, and the same applies to Tanaka Kakuei when I covered him.

The talent to read human mind precisely—I think this is an important condition to be a genius politician.

Inventor Edison said, "Genius is one percent inspiration and ninety-nine percent perspiration". Here "perspiration" means "efforts", telling that efforts are more important than anything else. At the same time, the one percent of "inspiration" is a border which distinguishes a genius and a ordinary person.

Miki Bukichi and Tanaka Kakuei, the geniuses of politics, had the "talent to read human mind precisely" and "inspiration". Nikai also has both of them. They are important conditions for a genius politician and might be an innate ability.

I truly hope Nikai will continue to act more energetically for the peace of Japan and the world.

Morita Minoru was born in 1932 in Ito, Shizuoka Prefecture. He graduated from the University of Tokyo's Engineering Department and, after holding such positions as the chief of publication department of Nihon Hyoron-Sya and the editor-in-chief of "Economic Seminar" magazine, got established as a political commentator in 1973. After that, he has been active in various areas such as radio, publication, and lectures. He is an honorary professor of Shandong University, a visiting professor of Higashi Nippon International University, and the director of "Morita Minoru Research Institute for the Global Civilization".

He has published many works, including ' 森田実の言わねばならぬ 名言123 選 ', ' 一期一縁 ', ' 公共事業必要論 ', ' 防災・減災に資する 国土強靱化政策が日本を救う！ ', ' 森田実の永田町政治に喝！ '. And he posts his essays on Facebook occasionally.

An Essay on Secretary-General Nikai Toshihiro：

A No.2 figure who surpasses No.1 figures /

A politician of peace, benevolence, and tolerance

First edition: 25 June 2021

Author: Morita Minoru

Publisher: Ronso-sha Co., Ltd.

Kitai Building 2F, 2-23, Kanda Jinbo-cho, Chiyoda-ku, Tokyo.

Tel: 03 (3264) 5254　Fax: 03 (3264) 5232

Designer: Munetoshi Jyun-ichi

Printing and Binding: Chuo-Seihan-Insatsu Co., Ltd.　Typesetting: Flex Art

ISBN 978-4-8460-2069-9

Copyright ©Morita Minoru, 2021　printed in Japan

二階俊博幹事長論

ナンバー１を越えたナンバー２実力者／平和・博愛・忠恕の政治家

森田実 著／2020年4月刊行
1091円＋税／四六判上製
ISBN 978-4-8460-1937-2

斬新な視点で描く、二階俊博の全体像。歴史は「ナンバー１ではなく、ナンバー２実力者を軸にして動く」とする著者が、《南方熊楠の和歌山魂と自由精神の継承者》である二階俊博の政治的業績を多角的に検証する。

二階俊博の新たな挑戦

森田実 著／2021年6月刊行
1091円＋税／四六判上製
ISBN 978-4-8460-2062-0

多角的な証言に支えられて、二階政治の原点は〈平和主義〉と〈郷土愛〉と喝破。平和・博愛・忠恕の政治家＝二階俊博は、コロナ危機を克服し、人類が安心して生活できる安全な社会を築くために、限りなき挑戦を続けているとする。